EXCEPTIONALITY, *12*(3), 127-128
Copyright © 2004, Taylor & Francis

PREFACE

Introduction to the Special Issue on Reading

The No Child Left Behind legislation signed into law in January 2002 provides guidelines for educational reform and accountability for all student learning. This legislation includes students with disabilities in all of its mandates including Reading First, statewide assessments, and annual progress reports. The rationale for the Reading First legislation is that students are not reading nearly well enough and that only 32% of fourth graders performed at or above the proficient achievement level in reading (Donahue, Finnegan, Lutkus, Allen, & Campbell, 2001). It is distressing that many of the students with low performance in reading represent students from low-income families and minorities.

We believe that research from the special education community provides an excellent resource of scientifically based reading research that can influence instruction for students with disabilities as well as other students at risk for reading difficulties. This special issue features the work of four researchers and their teams who have contributed to the excellent research base on reading practices for students with disabilities and those at risk for reading difficulties.

The first article discusses the importance of including expository text in reading comprehension instruction and outlines the effectiveness of instruction focused on how such text is structured. The authors, Joanna P. Williams, Kendra M. Hall, and Kristen D. Lauer, describe a study that indicates that children can benefit from text structure instruction as early as the second grade, and they also report the effects of intensive instruction on a compare and contrast expository structure.

The second article addresses vocabulary enhancement during storybook reading and is written by Michael D. Coyne, Deborah C. Simmons, Edward J. Kame'enui, and Michael Stoolmiller. This article provides the background on the importance of vocabulary development in reading comprehension and learning from text. These authors remind us of the importance of identifying and teaching vocabulary to young children to reduce the gap in their word knowledge but also as a valuable means of improving their ability to learn from text. In the experimental study reported in this article, they describe a vocabulary intervention that included storybook reading that improved students' word knowledge.

The third article, written by Eric Dion, Paul L. Morgan, Douglas Fuchs, and Lynn S. Fuchs, addresses the fact that even when reading instruction is generally effective, there are likely to be some children who do not respond. With a focus on the First-Grade Peer

Assisted Learning Strategies Reading Program, the authors discuss outcomes of empirically validated best practices. They then describe a study in which increasingly individualized and intensive interventions were given to nonresponders to improve their reading, and they conclude with a discussion of the implications of such efforts for special education service delivery.

The fourth article provides a conceptual framework of factors that need to be in place to support the effective development and implementation of professional development for teachers that will yield improved outcomes for their students' reading. This article, authored by David J. Chard, addresses the critical linkage between teacher's knowledge and skills and student outcomes.

We have learned a great deal from reading these articles. They provide a foundation for future research and implications for instruction.

REFERENCE

Donahue, P. L., Finnegan, R. J., Lutkus, A. D., Allen, N. L., & Campbell, J. R. (2001). *The nation's report card: Fourth-grade reading 2000* (Report No. NCES 2001–499). Washington, DC: U.S. Department of Education, Office of Educational Research and Improvement, National Center for Education Statistics.

Sharon Vaughn and Joanna P. Williams
Guest Editors

ARTICLES

Teaching Expository Text Structure to Young At-Risk Learners: Building the Basics of Comprehension Instruction

Joanna P. Williams
Department of Human Development
Teachers College, Columbia University

Kendra M. Hall
Department of Teacher Education
Brigham Young University

Kristen D. Lauer
Office of Special Education Programs
U.S. Department of Education

Expository text is often neglected in the elementary school curriculum even though most of the reading that children do in school is of that type. Most of the research that demonstrates the importance of text structure in reading comprehension and the benefits that accrue from instruction in text structure deals with children at or above the 4th grade. This research literature, reviewed briefly, provides the basis for the work that is described in this article, which involves younger children. First, a study is presented that demonstrates that children are sensitive to text structure, and therefore would benefit from instruction, as early as 2nd grade. Second, a new instructional program is described that focuses intensively on one specific expository structure, compare and contrast. Finally, the results of a study that evaluates the effects of the program are described.

When we think about the information that is contained in a text, we think primarily about information that relates to content. Indeed, most textual information is content information. Readers use that information to construct a meaningful mental representation of the

Requests for reprints should be sent to Joanna P. Williams, Department of Human Development, Box 238, Teachers College, Columbia University, 525 West 120th Street, New York, NY 10027. E-mail: jpw15@columbia.edu text and thereby comprehend it. However, some textual information concerns structure, not content. This structural information is important because it helps readers organize the content and thus aids in the process of constructing the mental representation, that is, the meaning of the text.

Text structure is inherent in a text's organizational pattern, which reflects the logical connections among the ideas in the text (Meyer, Brandt, & Bluth, 1980). These patterns are not limited to text; they represent general rhetorical structures (Dickson, Simmons, & Kame'enui, 1998; Weaver & Kintsch, 1991). There may be explicit markers in the surface text that guide the reader. Sometimes there are signal words such as *first* or *as a result,* which identify the particular genre of the text (narrative or expository) and the particular type of structure within a genre. There may also be titles or headings that cue the overall organization of the text. Sometimes there are no surface cues to the text's structure. However, proficient readers have a sense of the structures that exist. They can recognize them even in text that is not organized effectively. This knowledge helps them organize the information presented in text into a well-structured mental representation.

Many children, some who are just learning to read as well as some who are older, do not easily understand what they read. There may be many reasons for such difficulties, from inadequate decoding or fluency to a lack of task persistence. It is likely, however, that these problems are specifically a matter of poor comprehension, which often involves a lack of knowledge about text structure (Oakhill & Yuill, 1996).

In this article we first review briefly some of the research that demonstrates the importance of text structure in reading comprehension and the benefits that accrue from instruction. We focus on expository text and on studies relevant to children who are at risk for academic failure. Most of this work involves children at the fourth-grade level and above.

We then describe some of the work that we have done with younger children, second graders. We ask two questions. First, are students this young sensitive to text structure? Second, if they are, can we capitalize on this sensitivity and develop instruction in text structure that will improve their reading comprehension? We present a study that answers the first question in the affirmative. Then we describe a new instructional program that focuses intensively on one specific expository structure, compare and contrast, and we present the results of a study that evaluates the effects of this program. (It is intended that this short program might later be expanded to include a variety of expository text types.)

EXPOSITORY TEXT AND POOR READERS, INCLUDING READERS WITH LEARNING DISABILITIES

Although many children start school with an awareness of narrative text structure, few have an awareness of expository text structure. This is in part because most of the reading that parents do with their preschool children is from storybooks. This in turn is probably because expository text is more difficult; the relation between ideas that are presented in expository text is not the simple sequence of familiar events that are depicted in many narratives. Rather, they depict abstract logical relations (Stein & Trabasso, 1981).

Another reason why expository text is difficult to comprehend is that it appears in a variety of different organizational structures. Anderson and Armbruster (1984) listed six such structures: description, temporal sequence of events, explanation of concepts, definition and example, compare and contrast, and problem–solution–effect. Other authors (e.g., Meyer et al., 1980; Meyer et al., 2002) have similar lists. Moreover, most texts do not represent a single structure—they mix two or more of them (Meyer & Poon, 2001). Historical sequences exemplify a particularly common type of mixed structure, incorporating problem–solution–effect, description, and narrative (Perfetti, Britt, & Georgi, 1995).

Poor readers, including students with learning disabilities, find expository text structure particularly difficult. The earliest studies addressed the question of how well students were able to comprehend main ideas. Hansen (1978) found that students with learning disabilities did not recall as much main idea information as did normally achieving students, although both groups of students recalled comparable amounts of detail information. Wong's (1980) results were similar, but she also found that if prompting questions were provided, the two groups did equally well. Wong concluded that students with learning disabilities have particular difficulty organizing information on their own. However, it is not only poor readers and children with learning disabilities who have difficulties with expository text. In a study of children randomly drawn from suburban classrooms, Williams, Taylor, and deCani (1984) found that even the oldest students (seventh graders) were not sensitive to how the presence of anomalous information might modify a text's main idea.

Following these early studies, attention was soon drawn to a consideration of the several organizing structures that we have already described. Englert and Thomas (1987) compared normally developing students, students with learning disabilities, and students who were low achievers but who did not have learning disabilities. They looked at four types of expository text: description, enumeration, sequence, and compare and contrast. On a task that required the students to differentiate sentences that either related to the text topic or presented intrusive information, students demonstrated differential sensitivity to the four structures. There was greater sensitivity to the sequence structure than to the enumeration and description structures, which in turn showed greater sensitivity than the compare and contrast structure.

Englert and Thomas (1987) compared third and fourth graders with sixth and seventh graders, and they found that older students in all three student groups exhibited more sensitivity to structure, suggesting that awareness of text structure is developmental. When asked to identify inconsistencies in expository text content, the normally achieving students identified more inconsistencies than did the low-achieving students, who identified more than did the students with learning disabilities. Englert and Thomas concluded that poor readers could not use the interrelations in text to guide their comprehension. In addition, these students were not sensitive to their comprehension failures; they did not demonstrate any self-monitoring of their comprehension, for example, by going back to reread the text.

Several investigators have focused on problem–solution text, defined by Meyer et al. (1980) as including a description of a problem and the specification of a number of possible solutions that might solve the problem. This problem–solution structure fits a good portion of the content found in upper elementary history and social studies textbooks. It resembles narrative structure in that causal relations, which link actions in sequences, and motivational relations are found in both narratives and history textbooks (Black, 1985).

However, when Beck, McKeown, Sinatra, and Loxterman (1991) analyzed the structure of authentic history texts found in classrooms, they found that their causal event sequences are not presented in the same pattern as most narratives. Narratives typically follow a sequence that first presents the problem to be solved, then the action that solves the problem, and finally, an effect that occurs as a result of the action. Textbooks, on the other hand, often follow an action–effect–problem sequence. Beck et al. modified passages from authentic textbooks, reordering the content so that the passages followed a narrative sequence (problem–action–effect). They found that fourth- and fifth-grade students who read the revised texts recalled significantly more idea units and answered more questions correctly than did those who read the original textbook passages. These findings are often cited as clear evidence that text structure influences comprehension.

One outcome of such research findings is to provide motivation for writers to modify the organization of textbooks so that they conform to what we know about good (i.e., easy to understand) structure (Gersten, Fuchs, Williams, & Baker, 2001). However, that approach goes just so far. Students must be prepared for the many less-than-adequately structured texts that they will encounter both in and out of school.

A review by Dickson et al. (1998) describes 17 studies focused on the relation between text organization and comprehension; they concluded that knowledge of text organization affects comprehension especially in terms of the identification and recall of the most important information in a text. Good readers appear to be able to use this type of knowledge more effectively than poor readers.

INSTRUCTION

It might be expected that, given the documentation of students' difficulties with reading comprehension in general and with text structure in particular, there would be great efforts to provide suitable instruction. However, there have not been. There were a few research studies in the 1980s that focused on how best to teach text structure, but interest in the topic waned after a few years without having sparked any large-scale movement to apply the findings of the studies in the classroom.

Until 2 or 3 years ago there was almost a complete dearth of instruction focused on expository text in the early grades. In fact, there is little exposure to expository text in these grades. Hoffman et al. (1994) pointed out that basal readers typically include a very small proportion of expository text. Duke (2000), who examined 20 first-grade classrooms across 10 different school districts, found a scarcity of informational texts in all of them; she suggested that perhaps this lack of experience with expository text contributes to the fourth-grade slump in reading achievement noted by Chall, Jacobs, and Baldwin (1990). Without proper attention to expository text in the early grades, students remain unprepared for the comprehension demands that await them (Bernhardt, Destino, Kamil, & Rodriguez-Munoz, 1995; Jitendra, Edwards, Choutka, & Treadway, 2002).

There have been some research studies within the context of strategy instruction. Among the many strategies that have been recommended is one that teaches students about how text is structured, with the expectation that if they apply this knowledge as they read, their comprehension will improve (Gersten et al., 2001). However, on what basis would one decide which structure to teach? It seems reasonable to argue that students would profit from having instruction focused on a structure if they were at all sensitive to that structure, that is, if they responded differently to the same text content presented in well-structured form or in poorly structured form. Such sensitivity is often called *awareness,* but there is no implication that students are in any way conscious of their responses.

Richgels, McGee, Lomax, and Sheard (1987) found that sixth graders were indeed sensitive to and aware of text structure and also that their awareness varied as a function of structure type. Across five awareness and recall tasks, students were more consistently aware of a compare and contrast structure than a causation structure. Thus upper elementary school students are promising candidates for instruction in text structure.

Armbruster, Anderson, and Ostertag (1987) conducted an instructional study that dealt with a single structure, problem–solution. In their study, middle school students who were given explicit instruction in this structure recalled more information on an essay test than students who received more traditional instruction that included general comprehension questions and summarization. In addition, the structure-trained students identified more main ideas than did the other students, indicating that explicit instruction in structure facilitates the development of a well-structured mental representation.

Overall, the few instructional studies that exist, although far from conclusive, suggest that instruction, especially if geared to a single text structure, is effective in improving students' ability to comprehend expository text. Dickson (1999), for example, found that the compare and contrast structure could be taught successfully in middle school general education classrooms. Much more work in this area needs to be done. Very few instructional programs have been developed, and there is almost no work that focuses on the sustainability of effects over time or of generalization to structures different from the ones used in training.

In this review, we have cited several studies in which participants were children with learning disabilities. This is because much of this work was done by researchers in special education. More recently, researchers in general education have found that many of the difficulties exhibited by children with learning disabilities are also seen in poor readers who do not have learning disabilities. It also turns out that most of the instructional techniques first explored with students with learning disabilities can be of great help when developing instruction for other children at risk for academic failure.

A STUDY OF SECOND GRADERS' AWARENESS OF TEXT STRUCTURE

Are students at the second-grade level, who are just beginning to read independently, sensitive to text structure? If they are, we might capitalize on this sensitivity to develop instruction that would improve their reading comprehension.

We conducted a study (Lauer, 2002) in New York City public schools in which we worked with one type of expository text, problem–solution text. We followed up on Beck et al.'s (1991) finding that fourth- and sixth-grade students understood revised texts that followed the canonical narrative sequence (problem–action–effect) better than they understood the typical textbook sequence (action–effect–problem). We compared these two sequences to determine whether second graders were sensitive to text structure variations in the same way that older students were.

We also looked at content familiarity, another variable that has been shown to have powerful effects on reading comprehension in adults and older students (Alexander & Jetton, 2000). Many investigators have manipulated content familiarity by selecting a specific domain—baseball, for example—with which the participants are not familiar and then teaching half of the participants about the unknown domain; the participants who received instruction almost invariably comprehended novel text in that domain better than those who did not receive instruction (Pearson & Fielding, 1991).

We chose to focus instead on more general knowledge. Children become familiar with concepts, and they develop their knowledge of the world, through direct personal experience and also through vicarious experience, such as listening to stories and watching television. We wrote texts that had to do with actions and events that could likely occur in children's everyday lives, and we also wrote texts that depicted actions and events that do not commonly occur in their everyday lives. We had adults confirm that these texts involved generally familiar and generally unfamiliar content.

In comparing these two sets of texts, we were particularly interested in whether the variables of text structure and content familiarity would interact. The research on this point is very sparse. Taylor and Beach (1984) found that the structure of a text is useful only for readers for whom the content is unfamiliar; readers familiar with the content of a text do not have to rely on its structure to make sense of it. In contrast, McKeown, Beck, Sinatra, and Loxterman (1992) concluded that text structure helps when reading both familiar and unfamiliar texts.

Finally, we identified one additional variable of interest, reading comprehension ability. The range of comprehension skills within an elementary classroom is wide (Chambliss & Calfee, 1998), and we were interested in whether the effects of text structure and content familiarity differed for students who were proficient in comprehension ability and those who were not proficient.

Participants were second-grade students at risk for academic failure. Almost 90% of the students qualified for free or reduced-rate lunches, and 99% of them were minority students. They were randomly assigned to one of the two text structure conditions (narrative sequence and textbook sequence); all students received both familiar content texts and unfamiliar content texts. Reading ability (high and low) was determined on the basis of Woodcock Reading Mastery Passage Comprehension (Woodcock, 1998) subtest scores.

An example of our texts (in two of the four experimental versions) follows:

Narrative Sequence, Familiar Content
    Ann Wilson went to Food Land to buy food. She filled her grocery cart all the way to the top. When she got home, she worried about lifting the cart up the steps by herself. She lived on the third floor. She had to get her food to her apartment.

Ann saw a large piece of wood nearby. She put the wood over the steps. She used the wood as a ramp. Ann pushed the cart up the ramp. She got her groceries into her apartment.

History Textbook Sequence, Unfamiliar Content

George Eastman loved taking pictures. George read about taking pictures. He learned how to make film. He made the first film that did not need many liquids. He put his new film rolls in a much smaller camera. The cameras cost twenty-five dollars. A person could take a hundred pictures with these new cameras. It no longer took George a long time to make his film. Before, George had had to wet it. Then he had had to use other kinds of liquids. It had taken a long time and had been very messy.

After reading each text, students were queried. First they were asked to summarize the text. Next, they were asked four structure questions that were related to the important information in the text, phrased generically (Who is the paragraph about? What was wrong? What did the character do? What happened?). Then they were asked to summarize the paragraph again to see whether, after being exposed to the structure questions, they were more likely to include important information in their summary. Then they were asked detail questions for recall of unimportant information, and finally, content questions, which related to the important information. These content questions, unlike the structure questions, were phrased in terms of the specific content of the text.

We found that all three variables—text structure, content familiarity, and reading comprehension ability—affected performance. Moreover, the effects of each variable were independent of the effects of the other variables. The effects of each variable were different, however. High reading ability led to better performance on all tasks. Content familiarity helped the students answer questions concerning the important, but not the unimportant, content. Text structure helped them on a wider range of tasks—not only on the questions concerning important (but not unimportant) content but also on the summarization and resummarization tasks. That is, text structure helped them select important information to be included in their summaries. It helped on both familiar and unfamiliar content.

The fact that we found significant differences between texts structured in a history textbook sequence and texts structured in a narrative sequence demonstrated clearly that young readers at the second-grade level, including those both low and high in comprehension ability, are sensitive to expository text structure. This suggests that introducing expository text in the elementary grades, at least at Grade 2 and above, would be useful. This finding further suggests that if texts are to be used in history, social studies, and other content areas, it might be desirable to present them first in a narrative structure, which our young readers found easier to understand, than in the often-used history textbook structure. Following this type of introduction, a gradual introduction of the more challenging structure might be appropriate.

As expected, students comprehended texts about familiar events better than they comprehended texts about unfamiliar events. In addition, the two variables of text structure and content did not interact on any of our measures. Thus, a text that is structured effectively benefits both familiar and unfamiliar content.

It should be noted that our finding that there was no interaction between text structure and content familiarity might have been due to the particular type of text that we (and McKeown et al., 1992) used—text that contained a causal event structure. Taylor and Beach (1984), who did find an interaction, used texts that represented associations of concepts but not causality. In general, association texts are easier to comprehend than causal texts, as we learned from the Richgels et al. (1987) study. We are conducting further research to determine whether the type of text structure does in fact make a difference on this point.

THE TEXT STRUCTURE PROGRAM

Our findings also suggested that instruction in text structure might be undertaken profitably at the elementary level. We have developed an instructional program that emphasizes text structure as well as content, rather than content alone, as more traditional instruction does (Hall, 2002; Williams, in press). We again focused on a single but different structure, compare and contrast. Because evidence indicates that the students with whom we were working, second graders at risk for academic failure, benefit from intensive as well as systematic instruction (Gersten et al., 2001), we chose to use an explicit and structured instructional model that included explanation and modeling by the teacher, followed by guided and then independent practice (Williams, 1998).

Our instruction featured three strategies. First, students were taught how to use clue words to identify a text as a compare and contrast text. Second, they were taught how to use a graphic organizer to lay out the relevant information in the text. Third, they were taught a series of questions that would help them focus on the important information in the text.

Of course, even though our main purpose was to teach text structure, our program would inevitably be presenting content. We chose animal classification as the content; our goal was to teach students the characteristic features of each of the five classes of vertebrates (mammals, birds, fish, reptiles, and amphibians). To this end we selected five animals as prototypical examples of the five classes (lion, eagle, shark, crocodile, and frog). This content is included in the standards for elementary-level science curricula in New York State.

MATERIALS

The books we used included a comprehensive animal encyclopedia and a trade book about each of the five animals. In addition, we prepared short target paragraphs to be read and analyzed. Each of these paragraphs contained several comparative statements about two of the five animals; these statements presented the information that was the basis for categorizing them into the five vertebrate classes. These paragraphs became longer as the program proceeded. Toward the end of the program they also included some distractor information, that is, general information about the one or the other of the two animals that could not be put together with any other information in the paragraph to construct a comparative statement. Here are two examples of target paragraphs:

> Eagles and crocodiles are wild animals. Eagles are warm-blooded; however, crocodiles are cold-blooded. Eagles and crocodiles both lay eggs.

> Lions and sharks are interesting animals. Lions have hair covering their bodies, but sharks have scales. Sharks have fins to help them swim. Lions are warm-blooded; however, sharks are cold-blooded. Sharks get oxygen to breathe from the water, but lions get oxygen to breathe from the air. Lions live in groups called prides. Lions have babies; however, sharks lay eggs. Lions and sharks both have sharp teeth to help them hunt for food.

LESSONS

The program consisted of nine lessons, which were taught in 15 sessions. Each lesson focused on two of the five prototypical animals and contained the following sections: (a) clue words, (b) trade book reading and discussion, (c) vocabulary development, (d) reading and analysis of target paragraph, (e) graphic organizer, (f) compare and contrast strategy questions, (g) summary (with a paragraph frame as support), and (h) lesson review. The first lesson focused on two very familiar animals (cats and dogs) to help students practice the procedure without being distracted by new content.

Clue Words

At the beginning of each lesson, the teacher previewed the purpose of the lesson and introduced the eight clue words (*alike, both, and, compare, but, however, than,* and *contrast*). The teacher wrote the clue words on the board and elicited sentences that used one of the clue words.

Trade Book Reading and Discussion

During the next part of the lesson, teachers read to the class about the two animals from the encyclopedia and the trade books. Teachers then directed a discussion about the animals. This part of the lesson provided information about the animals beyond the specific information contained in the target paragraphs. It was also designed to heighten motivation—particularly important because difficulty in comprehending expository text may, in part, be attributed to lack of student interest (Armbruster et al., 1987).

Vocabulary Development

Teachers then introduced vocabulary concepts related to animal classification (*oxygen, hair, scales, feathers, warm-blooded,* and *cold-blooded*).

Reading and Analysis of a Target Paragraph

The students read the target paragraph silently, and then the teacher reread it as students followed along in their own copy. Students then analyzed the text to narrow in on the similarities and differences found in the paragraph. Students identified the individual sentences that represented the similarities and the differences. They then circled all the clue words. Finally, they took turns generating sentences that described how the two animals in the paragraph were the same or different. The teacher encouraged them to use well-structured comparative statements, that is, sentences that were based on accurate information from the paragraph and that included a clue word.

Graphic Organizer

Next, students organized the paragraph's content with the help of a matrix, the graphic organizer that best represents the compare and contrast structure (Calfee & Chambliss, 1987). An individual matrix was used for each animal feature that was compared in the paragraph. Students then wrote a well-structured comparative statement to match the content organized in the matrix. Paragraphs in earlier lessons contained less information (and therefore there were fewer matrices) than paragraphs in later lessons.

Compare and Contrast Questions

The students then organized the statements they had generated according to the following three questions: (a) What two things is this paragraph about? (b) How are they the same? and (c) How are they different?

Summary

Next, students wrote summaries of the paragraph. Summarization skills are complex, so students were provided with just a paragraph frame to use as a prompt. This structured approach to writing is particularly helpful to young children who are just beginning to develop their writing skills (Harris & Graham, 1996). In the later lessons no frame was provided.

Review

At the end of each lesson the teacher and students reviewed the vocabulary and the strategies (clue words, graphic organizer, and compare and contrast questions).

EVALUATION OF THE INSTRUCTIONAL PROGRAM

We evaluated the effectiveness of our program by comparing it to a program that was more traditional in orientation and that did not emphasize text structure. Both programs covered the same content. As a control, we also looked at students who received neither program. The main purpose of the study was to determine whether instruction focused on text structure helps second-grade students improve their comprehension of compare and contrast expository text. We also had a further question. The school day contains a finite amount of time, and choices must be made as to what to spend that time on. If teaching students about text structure means that they will learn less content, then we must understand that, and we must be prepared to make a trade-off. However, there might be no diminution of content learning, which would be a better outcome. Therefore we asked whether this type of instruction on text structure would detract from students' ability to learn new content.

Teachers of 10 second-grade classes in three New York City public schools volunteered to participate in the program. All but one of the teachers had master's degrees. We randomly assigned the 10 intact classes to one of the three treatments (text structure, $n = 4$; content, $n = 4$; and no instruction, $n = 2$).

A total of 128 students participated. Across the three schools, the enrollment included approximately 56% Hispanic children, 41% African American, 2% Caucasian, and 1% Asian. Almost 90% of the children received state aid in the form of free or reduced-rate lunch. Approximately 6% of the students were enrolled in special education services.

The Content Program

The comparison content program was designed to correspond to more traditional content-area instruction and was intended to be a viable program. We expected that students participating in this program would learn important content that would enable them to comprehend novel paragraphs about similar content.

The materials for this program, that is, the actual texts used (encyclopedia, trade books, and target paragraphs) were the same as those used in the text structure program. As in the other program, there were 15 sessions, so that overall the same amount of time was given to the instruction. Each lesson consisted of the following sections: (a) background knowledge, (b) trade book reading and discussion, (c) information web (a graphic organizer that organizes information topically), (d) vocabulary development, (e) reading of target paragraph, (f) general content discussion, (g) summary (with paragraph frame), and (h) lesson review.

RESULTS OF THE INSTRUCTIONAL STUDY

Strategy Measures

Following the lessons, we interviewed students individually, asking them to respond to questions both orally and in writing. First, we wanted to determine whether they had learned the three strategies that we taught them. Several measures evaluated the acquisition of the strategies taught in the text structure program. We assessed recall of clue words, the ability to identify the clue words in a paragraph, the ability to generate sentences (oral and written) based on information they had graphically organized, and finally, recall of the three compare and contrast questions. On the first three of these measures, the students who received the text structure instruction did significantly better than the students in the other two groups. On the fourth measure, recall of the three compare and contrast questions, there was no effect of treatment.

The comparison content program included one strategy, a graphic organizer (i.e., an information web). There were no differences among the three treatment groups in their proficiency in this strategy. All groups achieved relatively high scores, indicating second graders' familiarity with the web strategy.

Outcome Measures

Next, we turned our attention to outcome measures. Did the students really improve in their ability to apply what they had learned? There were two types of outcome measures. The first type addressed the text structure goals of the study; these measures assessed students' ability to gain information from expository text. The second type evaluated the content, the specific information about animals that the students had learned from the instructional program.

First, what was learned about text structure? We first looked at the students' ability to summarize a compare and contrast paragraph that contained material explicitly taught in the program, that is, information about two of the five instructed animals. The test paragraph compared two animals that had been directly compared during the instruction. We asked for written summaries. We counted the number of summary statements that were accurate and that included an appropriate clue word. The text structure group performed better than did the other two groups.

Then we investigated the students' ability to transfer. The goal of reading comprehension instruction is to have students improve in their ability to read novel content, not simply to reread material that they have already practiced. Therefore we developed a series of three compare and contrast texts that were structured in the same way as those used in the instruction. However, the content was different. In each of these three paragraphs, the content became further removed from the content used in the instruction.

First, we wrote a paragraph that contained information about two of the instructed animals but two that had not been directly compared in any of the lesson target paragraphs (sharks and crocodiles). We considered this a measure of what was explicitly taught in the program. The second paragraph contained information concerning the animal classification of two animals that had not been mentioned during the instruction (elephants and turtles). This we considered a measure of near transfer. The last paragraph in the series contained information unrelated to animal classification; it compared bikes and cars. We considered this a measure of far transfer. Here, we asked for oral summaries. We found that across the three paragraphs, the text structure group scored significantly higher than either of the other two groups not only on the instructed paragraph but also on the transfer paragraphs. These findings indicated that the text structure students had in fact transferred what they had learned.

We were pleased with these results. It is not uncommon to find that after reading comprehension instruction, students do better on tests that involve the same material on which they were instructed. However, it is less common to find positive effects of the instruction when the tests involve new material not seen during instruction.

Now let us turn to the second type of outcome measure, which focused on how much of the content about animals had been learned. We were interested in two types of content learning. First, did the students learn the vocabulary concepts (e.g., *oxygen* and *warm-blooded*) that we taught them? They did. Here, we found a different pattern of results from what we found on the text structure outcome measures: The text structure group attained a higher score on the vocabulary measure than did the content group, but in addition, the content group did better than the no-treatment control group. In our other content outcome measures, we asked the students one detail question about each of the five target animals. These questions tapped information that was presented in the read-alouds that were the basis for the class discussions. On this measure, there was no effect of instructional group.

These findings concerning the amount of content learned are important because they indicate that spending substantial instructional time on text structure training did not detract from the amount of content the students learned. The content group, whose instruction focused solely on content, did not acquire more information about animals than the text structure group.

Our final outcome measure looked at transfer of another variety. We have described our assessment of transfer to new content; here we describe our assessment of the students' ability to transfer to a new text structure. Our question was, if second graders are given highly structured, very intensive training in one text structure, will they also read and comprehend another type of expository text better than noninstructed students will?

We wrote a paragraph that followed a pro–con structure; it included arguments for and against animals in zoos. Both the compare and contrast and the pro–con strategies conform to an associative structure (different from a problem–solution or causality structure). We asked the children to read the paragraph and to give us an oral summary; there were no differences among the three instructional groups. These results indicate that instruction in one particular text structure does not necessarily transfer to other text structures, even if they are related.

DIFFERENCES IN RESPONSIVENESS TO INSTRUCTION

Positive findings based on comparisons of classroom means are certainly important, but we should also look further, beyond mean differences. Given the fact that more and more schools are moving toward an inclusion model in which students having widely disparate achievement levels receive their instruction together in one classroom, it is important to find out how well individual children are responding to the instruction. It is especially important to determine whether the children with special education status are responding satisfactorily to the regular classroom curriculum. Therefore we looked to see what the characteristics were of children who did not make much progress in our program.

We decided that a child who, having gone through our text structure instruction, did not apply the strategies he or she was taught or did not transfer them to novel texts would be considered a nonresponder (Al Otaiba & Fuchs, 2002). On the basis of certain posttest outcome measures, we categorized the participants as either responders or non-responders. We established two sets of criteria for acceptable performance on these measures, one stringent and the other more lenient. Regardless of which criteria we used, we found, not surprisingly, that the students who had not performed as well as the others had lower listening and lower reading comprehension scores. However, there was no relation between nonresponding and special education status. That is, it was no more likely that a student with an individualized education plan or a referral for one would be a nonresponder than a student who was in neither of these categories.

CONCLUSIONS

Overall, our study demonstrated that text structure instruction helps students improve their comprehension of compare and contrast expository text. Moreover, it does so without detracting from the ability to learn new content. It should be noted that posttest scores indicated that there was still a great deal of room for growth. It is likely that the students might have benefited from more instruction than we provided—even though what we gave them was well in excess of what they receive in the typical classroom. Nevertheless, the effect sizes were substantial, indicating that as early as second grade, students do respond positively to text structure instruction.

Our work has suggested further questions. The study should be replicated with other types of content, for example, social studies. We also want to pursue the question of whether young children should be given intensive instruction specifically in each of the several expository text structures. Although we found good transfer to content not used in the instruction, we did not find transfer to another text structure, pro–con, that was not used in training. Given the importance of comprehending expository text, it is crucial that students be provided with instruction that will prepare them to deal with whatever type of text they encounter.

Duke, Bennett, Armistead, and Roberts (2002) have spoken eloquently about the lack of exposure to expository text in the primary grades. We echo their concern. In fact, we believe that children in the early grades would benefit from explicit instruction in expository text structure; it would provide a good preparation for the challenging reading tasks that they will face in middle and high school and throughout their lives.

ACKNOWLEDGMENTS

This article was cowritten by Kristen D. Lauer in her private capacity. No official support or endorsement by the U.S. Department of Education is intended or should be inferred.

REFERENCES

Alexander, P. A., & Jetton, T. L. (2000). Learning from text: A multidimensional and developmental perspective. In M. L. Kamil, P. B. Mosenthal, P. D. Pearson, & R. Barr (Eds.), *Handbook of reading research* (Vol. 3, pp. 285–310). Mahwah, NJ: Lawrence Erlbaum Associates, Inc.

Al Otaiba, S., & Fuchs, D. (2002). Characteristics of children who are unresponsive to early literacy intervention. *Remedial and Special Education, 23,* 300–316.

Anderson, T. H., & Armbruster, B. B. (1984). Content area textbooks. In R. C. Anderson, J. Osborn, & R. J. Tierney (Eds.), *Learning to read in American schools* (pp. 193–226). Hillsdale, NJ: Lawrence Erlbaum Associates, Inc.

Armbruster, B. B., Anderson, T. H., & Ostertag, J. (1987). Does text structure/summarization instruction facilitate learning from expository text? *Reading Research Quarterly, 22,* 331–346.

Beck, I. L., McKeown, M. G., Sinatra, G. M., & Loxterman, J. A. (1991). Revising social studies text from a text-processing perspective: Evidence of improved comprehensibility. *Reading Research Quarterly, 26,* 251–276.

Bernhardt, E., Destino, T., Kamil, M., & Rodriguez-Munoz, M. (1995). Assessing science knowledge in an English–Spanish bilingual elementary school. *Cognosos, 4,* 4–6.

Black, J. B. (1985). Prose analysis: Purposes, procedures, and problems. In B. K. Britton & J. B. Black (Eds.), *Understanding expository texts: A theoretical and practical handbook for analyzing explanatory text* (pp. 249–267). Hillsdale, NJ: Lawrence Erlbaum Associates, Inc.

Calfee, R. C., & Chambliss, M. J. (1987). Structural design features of large texts. *Educational Psychologist, 22,* 357–378.

Chall, J. S., Jacobs, V. A., & Baldwin, L. E. (1990). *The reading crisis: Why poor children fall behind.* Cambridge, MA: Harvard University Press.

Chambliss, M. J., & Calfee, R. C. (1998). *Textbooks for learning.* Malden, MA: Blackwell.

Dickson, S. (1999). Integrating reading and writing to teach compare–contrast text structure: A research-based methodology. *Reading & Writing Quarterly, 14,* 49–79.

Dickson, S., Simmons, D. C., & Kame'enui, E. J. (1998). Text organization: Research bases. In D. C. Simmons & E. J. Kame'enui (Eds.), *What reading research tells us about children with diverse learning needs* (pp. 239–277). Mahwah, NJ: Lawrence Erlbaum Associates, Inc.

Duke, N. K. (2000). 3.6 minutes per day: The scarcity of informational texts in first grade. *Reading Research Quarterly, 35,* 202–224.

Duke, N. K., Bennett-Armistead, V. S., & Roberts, E. M. (2002). Incorporating informational text in the primary grades. In C. M. Roller (Ed.), *Comprehensive reading instruction across grade levels: A collection of papers from Reading Research 2001 Conference* (pp. 40–54). Newark, DE: International Reading Association.

Englert, C. S., & Thomas, C. C. (1987). Sensitivity to text structure in reading and learning: A comparison between learning disabled and non-learning disabled students. *Learning Disability Quarterly, 10*(2), 93–105.

Gersten, R., Fuchs, L. S., Williams, J. P., & Baker, S. (2001). Teaching reading comprehension strategies to students with learning disabilities: A review of research. *Review of Educational Research, 71,* 279–320.

Hall, K. M. (2002). *A study of the effect of text structure and content on at-risk second graders' comprehension of compare/contrast expository text.* Unpublished doctoral dissertation, Columbia University, New York.

Hansen, C. L. (1978). Story retelling used with average and learning disabled readers as a measure of reading comprehension. *Learning Disability Quarterly, 1,* 62–69.

Harris, K. R., & Graham, S. (1996). *Making the writing process work: Strategies for composition and self-regulation.* Cambridge, MA: Brookline Books.

Hoffman, J. V., McCarthy, S. J., Abbott, J., Christian, C., Corman, L., Curry, C., et al. (1994). So what's new in the new basals? A focus on first grade. *Journal of Reading Behavior, 26,* 47–73.

Jitendra, A. K., Edwards, L. L., Choutka, C. M., & Treadway, P. S. (2002). A collaborative approach to planning in the content areas for students with learning disabilities: Accessing the general curriculum. *Learning Disabilities Research & Practice, 17,* 252–267.

Lauer, K. D. (2002). *The effect of text structure, content familiarity, and reading ability on second-graders' comprehension of text.* Unpublished doctoral dissertation, Columbia University, New York.

McKeown, M. G., Beck, I. L., Sinatra, G. M., & Loxterman, J. A. (1992). The contribution of prior knowledge and coherent text to comprehension. *Reading Research Quarterly, 27,* 79–93.

Meyer, B. J. F., Brandt, D. M., & Bluth, G. J. (1980). Use of top-level structure in text: Key for reading comprehension of ninth-grade students. *Reading Research Quarterly, 16,* 72–103.

Meyer, B. J. F., & Poon, L. W. (2001). Effects of the structure strategy and signaling on recall of text. *Journal of Educational Psychology, 93,* 141–159.

Meyer, B. J. F., Theodorou, E., Brezenski, K. L., Middlemiss, W., McDougall, J., & Bartlett, B. J. (2002). Effects of structure strategy instruction delivered to fifth-grade children using the Internet with and without the aid of older adult tutors. *Journal of Educational Psychology, 94,* 486–519.

Oakhill, J., & Yuill, N. (1996). Higher order factors in comprehension disability: Processes and remediation. In C. Cornoldi & J. Oakhill (Eds.), *Reading comprehension difficulties* (pp. 69–92). Mahwah, NJ: Lawrence Erlbaum Associates, Inc.

Pearson, P. D., & Fielding, L. (1991). Comprehension instruction. In R. Barr, M. L. Kamil, P. Mosenthal, & P. D. Pearson (Eds.), *Handbook of reading research* (Vol. 3, pp. 815–860). New York: Longman.

Perfetti, C. A., Britt, M. A., & Georgi, M. C. (1995). *Text-based learning and reasoning: Studies in history.* Hillsdale, NJ: Lawrence Erlbaum Associates, Inc.

Richgels, D. J., McGee, L. M., Lomax, R. G., & Sheard, C. (1987). Awareness of four text structures: Effects on recall of expository text. *Reading Research Quarterly, 22,* 177–196.

Stein, N. L., & Trabasso, T. (1981). What's in a story: An approach to comprehension and instruction. In R. Glaser (Ed.), *Advances in instructional psychology* (Vol. 2, pp. 213–267). Hillsdale, NJ: Lawrence Erlbaum Associates. Inc.

Taylor, B. M., & Beach, R. W. (1984). The effects of text structure instruction on middle grade students comprehension and production of expository text. *Reading Research Quarterly, 19,* 134–146.

Weaver, C. A., & Kintsch, W. (1991). Expository text. In R. Barr, M. L. Kamil, P. Mosenthal, & P. D. Pearson (Eds.), *Handbook of reading research* (Vol. 2, pp. 230–244). White Plains, NY: Longman.

Williams, J. P. (1998). Improving the comprehension of disabled readers. *Annals of Dyslexia, 48,* 213–238.

Williams, J. P. (in press). Instruction in reading comprehension for primary-grade students: A focus on text structure. *Journal of Special Education.*

Williams, J. P., Taylor, M. B., & deCani, J. S. (1984). Constructing macrostructure for expository text. *Journal of Educational Psychology, 76,* 1065–1075.

Wong, B. Y. L. (1980). Activating the inactive learner: Use of questions/prompts to enhance comprehension and retention of implied information in learning disabled children. *Learning Disability Quarterly, 3,* 29–37.

Woodcock, R. N. (1998). *Woodcock Reading Mastery Tests—Revised.* Circle Pines, MN: American Guidance Service.

Teaching Vocabulary During Shared Storybook Readings: An Examination of Differential Effects

Michael D. Coyne
Department of Educational Psychology
University of Connecticut

Deborah C. Simmons
Department of Educational Psychology
Texas A&M University

Edward J. Kame'enui
Institute for the Development of Educational Achievement
University of Oregon

Michael Stoolmiller
University of Oregon, and
Northern Michigan University

A storybook intervention for kindergarten children that integrates principles of explicit vocabulary instruction within the shared storybook reading experience is described with findings from an experimental study demonstrating the effects of this intervention on the vocabulary development of kindergarten students at risk of reading difficulty. Results indicated that in comparison to students in the control group, students in the intervention with lower receptive vocabulary skills demonstrated greater gains in explicitly taught vocabulary than did students with higher receptive vocabulary. Findings suggest that the explicit teaching of word meanings within storybook readings may help to narrow, or at least halt, the widening vocabulary gap among students.

Beginning reading research has converged on a profound and irrefutable finding over the past decade: Children enter kindergarten with "meaningful differences" in early literacy experiences (Hart & Risley, 1995). Even at this early age, children's literacy development and opportunities are characterized by differences in skills, exposure, and opportu-

---

Requests for reprints should be sent to Michael D. Coyne, Department of Educational Psychology, 249 Glenbrook Road #2064, Neag School of Education, University of Connecticut, Storrs, CT 06269. E-mail: mike.coyne@uconn.edu

nities with the form, functions, and conventions of language and print (National Research Council, 1998).

For example, young children differ considerably in their understanding of and familiarity with the phonologic features of language and the alphabetic nature of our writing system (Torgesen et al., 1999). Whereas some children come to school having already grasped the insight that language can be broken down into individual phonemes that map onto letters, many other children have only the most rudimentary awareness of sounds and print. A large body of research evidence suggests that these differences in phonological awareness and letter knowledge have important implications for learning to read and predicting success in beginning reading acquisition (Foorman & Torgesen, 2001; National Reading Panel, 2000).

Similarly, young children possess vastly divergent vocabularies (Biemiller, 2001; Hart & Risley, 1995; National Research Council, 1998). Whereas some children enter school with thousands of hours of exposure to books and a wealth of rich oral language experiences, other children begin school with very limited knowledge of language and word meanings. Like the research base on phonological awareness and alphabetic understanding, teachers and researchers have long recognized the important and prominent role that vocabulary knowledge plays in becoming a successful reader (Becker, 1977; Cunningham & Stanovich, 1998; National Reading Panel, 2000; Storch & Whitehurst, 2002).

The research evidence is unequivocal: Children enter kindergarten with significant differences in critical early literacy skills, and these differences place many children at serious risk for failing to learn how to read and understand text. As a result, early intervention matters, and it matters more for children who enter with less. These children not only begin school with limited skills and knowledge, but also these initial differences grow larger and more discrepant over time (Biemiller, 2003; Stanovich, 1986). The goal of early intervention, therefore, is to target differences in early literacy skills and experiences at the outset of formal schooling before reading difficulties become entrenched and intractable (Coyne, Kame'enui, & Simmons, 2001). To this end, educators, policymakers, and researchers have actively and increasingly promoted prevention and early intervention efforts in beginning reading (e.g., No Child Left Behind, 2002).

The results of early intervention have been largely encouraging. Over the past 10 years, researchers have engaged in a concerted and ever more successful effort to develop effective instructional strategies and interventions to increase the phonological awareness and word identification skills of young children at risk for reading difficulties and disability (e.g., Foorman, Francis, Fletcher, Schatschneider, & Mehta, 1998; Simmons et al., 2004; Torgesen et al., 1999). Yet, even as the research community has concentrated its collective attention on helping children read words, there has been very little corresponding research recently on helping children understand words or develop equally critical vocabulary knowledge. This is particularly true for students in the early grades (National Reading Panel, 2000). As Biemiller and Slonim (2001) recently asserted: "Although vocabulary development is crucial for school success, it has not received the attention and interest that work on identifying printed words and spelling have received" (p. 511).

There is a need for research-based, intensive vocabulary interventions for young children at risk of experiencing reading difficulties. To address this need, we developed and evaluated an intervention that integrated knowledge from two complementary research literatures: the storybook literature and the vocabulary literature. In developing the intervention, we incorporated validated principles of explicit and systematic vocabulary instruction from research conducted with students in Grades 3 and above (Beck, McKeown, & Kucan, 2002) into storybook reading activities typically used with children in preschool through Grade 2.

In this article, we summarize the research on storybook and shared book reading activities followed by the literature base on direct vocabulary instruction. Next, we describe a storybook intervention for kindergarten children that integrates principles of explicit vocabulary instruction within the shared storybook reading experience. We then summarize findings from an experimental study demonstrating the effects of this intervention on the vocabulary development of kindergarten students at risk of reading disability. In addition, we present secondary analyses that examine whether there were differential effects of the intervention for students who began kindergarten with low receptive vocabulary skills.

SHARED STORYBOOK READING ACTIVITIES
IN PRESCHOOL TO GRADE 2

Older students in third grade and above acquire a great deal of new vocabulary through wide, independent reading (Anderson & Nagy, 1992). Younger students who have yet to become skilled readers, however, must learn word meanings through a different medium (Becker, 1977). The primary way for young nonreaders to be exposed to new vocabulary is within the context of oral language experiences such as shared storybook reading (Biemiller, 2003). Storybook reading activities are an excellent means for language and vocabulary development because of the opportunities for using decontextualized language during interactive discussion (Snow, 1991) and the relative rarity of the vocabulary encountered in storybooks compared with speech (Cunningham & Stanovich, 1998). For example, the complexity of vocabulary found in children's books is greater than in all of adult conversation, except for courtroom testimony (Hayes & Ahrens, 1988).

There is a growing literature documenting the effects of listening to storybooks on language and vocabulary development (Bus, van Ijzendoorn, & Pellegrini, 1995; National Reading Panel, 2000). For example, studies have found that children can learn the meanings of unknown words through incidental exposure during shared storybook reading activities (Elley, 1989; Nicholson & Whyte, 1992; Robbins & Ehri, 1994; Senechal & Cornell, 1993).

Researchers have begun to isolate factors that increase the likelihood that children will learn new vocabulary from listening to storybooks. These factors include engaging in rich dialogic discussion about the storybook (Senechal, 1997; Whitehurst, Epstein, et al., 1994; Whitehurst et al., 1999), reading storybooks multiple times (Robbins & Ehri, 1994; Senechal, Thomas, & Monker, 1995), providing performance-oriented readings (Dickinson & Smith, 1994), and reading storybooks with small groups of students (Whitehurst, Arnold, et al., 1994). Finally, it is important to choose engaging storybooks with beautiful pictures and appealing stories that will capture and hold children's interest and attention.

The results of these studies suggest that shared storybook reading activities are a valuable way to support vocabulary development in young children. However, evidence also reveals that these activities are not equally effective for all students. Children who are at risk for reading difficulties with lower initial vocabularies are less likely to learn unknown words from incidental exposure during storybook reading activities than their peers with higher vocabularies (Nicholson & Whyte, 1992; Robbins & Ehri, 1994; Senechal et al., 1995). In other words, with traditional storybook reading activities, the initial vocabulary differences among students grow larger over time (Penno, Wilkinson, & Moore, 2002; Stanovich, 1986).

In response to this finding, researchers have called recently for more conspicuous, teacher-directed vocabulary instruction to complement traditional storybook reading activities for young children who are at risk for experiencing reading difficulties (Biemiller & Slonim, 2001; Simmons et al., 2004; Stahl & Shiel, 1999). For example, Robbins and Ehri (1994) concluded that "because children with weaker vocabularies are less likely to learn new words from listening to stories than children with larger vocabularies, teachers need to provide more explicit vocabulary instruction for children with smaller vocabularies" (p. 61).

The goal of our intervention was to intensify shared book reading activities with direct teaching of target vocabulary. To accomplish this, we looked to a separate but related knowledge base, the research on explicit vocabulary instruction (Baumann, Kame'enui, & Ash, 2003; Beck et al., 2002). In the next section, we summarize the vocabulary instructional literature.

EXPLICIT VOCABULARY INSTRUCTION
IN GRADES 3 AND ABOVE

Although there is little research on explicit vocabulary instruction in kindergarten through Grade 2, there is a more extensive literature on direct vocabulary instruction in Grades 3 and above (Baker, Simmons, & Kame'enui, 1998; Baumann et al., 2003). There is especially strong evidence regarding the effectiveness of explicit vocabulary instruction that focuses on teaching students the meanings of specific words and instructional principles that maximize vocabulary learning (National Reading Panel, 2000).

Explicit vocabulary instruction should directly teach the meanings of words that are important for understanding the text and words that children will encounter often (Stahl, 1986). Effective strategies for directly teaching vocabulary include using both contextual and definitional information, giving multiple exposures of target words, and encouraging deep processing (National Reading Panel, 2000; Stahl, 1986; Stahl & Fairbanks, 1986). Activities that encourage deep processing challenge students to move beyond memorizing simple dictionary definitions to understanding words at a richer, more complex level by, for example, describing how they relate to other words and to their own experiences (McKeown & Beck, 2003).

Direct instruction of target words is also more effective when it adheres to validated principles of instructional and curricular design (Kame'enui, Carnine, Dixon, Simmons, & Coyne, 2002). For example, vocabulary instruction should be conspicuous (Baker et al., 1998). Conspicuous instruction is explicit and unambiguous and consists of carefully designed and delivered teacher actions. During vocabulary instruction, this would include direct presentations of word meanings using clear and consistent wording and extensive teacher modeling of new vocabulary in multiple contexts. Vocabulary instruction should also provide students with carefully scheduled review and practice to help them more firmly incorporate new vocabulary into their lexicon (Baker et al., 1998).

The vocabulary instruction literature has important implications for younger students at risk of reading difficulties. Previously, many researchers have argued that the number of words that children need to learn is so great that the role of direct instruction in helping children develop vocabulary knowledge is insignificant and inconsequential (Anderson & Nagy, 1992). Recently, however, other researchers have begun to question this assertion. Lower estimates of the number of root-word meanings that typical students acquire in a year suggest that direct instruction can, in fact, provide students with a significant proportion of words they will learn, especially students with less developed vocabularies (Biemiller, 2003; Stahl & Shiel, 1999).

To date, most research on explicit vocabulary instruction has been carried out with children in Grade 3 and above (e.g., Beck, Perfetti, & McKeown, 1982; Kame'enui, Carnine, & Freschi, 1982; McKeown, Beck, Omanson, & Perfetti, 1983). Unfortunately, waiting until third grade to address vocabulary development for students with low vocabularies systematically may be too late for children who enter school at risk for experiencing reading difficulties. The urgency of targeting vocabulary development in the early grades was made acutely apparent in recent research conducted by Biemiller and Slonim (2001). Their findings revealed that most of the vocabulary differences between children occur before Grade 3, at which point children with high vocabularies know thousands of more word meanings than children who are experiencing delays in vocabulary development.

In summary, research highlights the need for early interventions that offer effective classroom-based vocabulary instruction for young children at risk of experiencing reading difficulties. The two distinct research literatures outlined previously provide a conceptual and empirical basis for developing such an intervention by incorporating validated principles of explicit and systematic vocabulary instruction from research conducted with students in Grades 3 and above into storybook reading activities for young children in kindergarten through Grade 2. In the following section, we describe a storybook intervention informed by this conceptual framework.

AN EXPERIMENTAL STORYBOOK INTERVENTION

We are currently engaged in a longitudinal program of research to investigate ways to optimize early literacy instruction and intervention for children at risk of reading difficulties (Simmons et al., 2004; Simmons, Kame'enui, Stoolmiller, Coyne, & Harn, 2003). This research is guided by two primary questions: (a) What are the critical components of early literacy instruction and how should we allocate instructional time among these literacy components? and (b) To what extent does instruction that is sufficiently explicit, systematic, and strategic meet the intensive literacy needs of children at risk of reading difficulty?

As part of this larger program of research, we developed a storybook intervention to increase children's vocabulary knowledge and enhance their comprehension, two critical components of early literacy instruction. When designing the elements of the intervention targeting vocabulary development, we explicitly incorporated and integrated the instructional principles distilled from our review of the storybook and vocabulary research. To make the linkage between the research principles and their application more transparent, we outline these connections in two tables. Table 1 summarizes the research principles gleaned from the shared storybook reading literature and how we incorporated them into our intervention. Table 2 summarizes our application of the research principles synthesized from the vocabulary instruction literature.

The intervention consisted of 108 half-hour lessons developed to accompany 40 children's storybooks. The storybooks were either classics or recent award winners. Three target vocabulary words to be taught explicitly were identified from each storybook. Target words were selected because they were important for understanding the story and likely to be unfamiliar to young children.

Lessons were sequenced in 20, six-day cycles. Each cycle was designed to complement two storybooks. One storybook was read on Days 1 and 3 of the cycle and the other storybook was read on Days 2 and 4. Days 5 and 6 focused on integrating and applying target vocabulary to generalized contexts. During Days 5 and 6, children were also given opportunities to retell the stories using selected illustrations as prompts. Teachers encouraged children to use target vocabulary during retells.

We evaluated the effects of our storybook intervention within the context of a large-scale experimental study with kindergarten children identified as at risk of experi-

TABLE 1
Shared Storybook Reading Literature

Research Principle	Application
Interesting and engaging storybooks	Storybooks chosen were either classics (e.g., *Bread and Jam for Francis, Harry the Dirty Dog*) or recent award winners (e.g., *Hush! A Thai Lullaby, McDuff Moves In*).
Rich dialogic discussion about storybooks	Teachers engaged children in scaffolded discussion of the story by activating prior knowledge, eliciting responses about story elements, linking story themes to children's own experiences, and facilitating story recalls.
Performance-oriented readings	Discussion took place primarily before and after story readings. Teachers read stories with expression and enthusiasm.
Multiple readings of storybooks	Storybooks were read two times over four lessons. Students also retold each story one additional time with prompted connections to the storybook's illustrations.
Small groups of students	Storybooks were read with groups of 2 to 5 children.

TABLE 2
Vocabulary Instruction Literature

Research Principle	Application
Carefully selected target words	Three target words were chosen and taught directly from each storybook. Words were selected because they were important to understanding the story and likely to be unfamiliar to kindergarten students.
Simple definitions within the context of the story	Teachers provided students with a simple definition or synonym (e.g., "*rumpus* means wild play") when introducing a new vocabulary word. Teachers then used the definition within the context of the story. In the story *Where the Wild Things Are,* for example, the teacher says, "I'll say the sentence with the words that mean the same as *rumpus.* 'Let the wild play start.'"
Conspicuous instruction	Definitions of target words were presented through instruction that was direct and unambiguous. Definitions were explicitly modeled by teachers using clear and consistent wording.
Rich instruction	Teachers provided children opportunities to discuss target words in extended discourse before and after stories. In addition, teachers provided children with structured discrimination and generalization tasks that challenged them to process word meanings at a deeper and more complex level (e.g., "Is *rumpus* more like sitting quietly or wild play?" "Have you ever been in a *rumpus*?").
Multiple exposures to target words and carefully scheduled review and practice	Target vocabulary words were introduced and reviewed a minimum of 6 days in a carefully scaffolded sequence. Each target word was first used by the teacher in context, practiced in sentences by students, incorporated into story recalls, and discussed in multiple novel contexts.

encing reading difficulties (Simmons et al., 2004). The kindergarten children were considered to be at risk based on their performance on letter naming and phonological awareness tasks administered at the beginning of the school year (Good, Simmons, & Kame'enui, 2001; Torgesen, 2000).

In November of the kindergarten year, 96 children from seven schools were randomly assigned to one of three intervention groups. Only one of the three groups received the storybook intervention. A second group received an intervention that focused on increasing phonologic and alphabetic skills, two other critical components of early literacy instruction. The remaining control group received a sounds and letters module of a commercial reading program (Open Court; Adams et al., 2000). Children in all groups received 30 min of small group intervention each day between November and May for a total of 108 instructional periods.

As expected, the group receiving the code-based instruction outperformed the storybook and control groups on measures of phonologic and alphabetic skills. However, the storybook group scored significantly higher than the code-based and control groups at posttest on an experimenter-developed, expressive measure of explicitly taught vocabulary. Effect sizes for these contrasts were moderate to large. The effect size for the storybook group in contrast with the code-based group was $d = .73$ and the effect size for the storybook group in contrast with the control group was $d = .85$.

Results of this study suggested two primary conclusions (Simmons et al., 2004). First, because learning to read involves the complex interaction of multiple skills and strategies, sufficient instructional time should be allocated to each of the critical components of early literacy instruction. As predicted, the intervention that targeted code-based components produced large effects on children's phonologic and alphabetic skills, whereas the intervention that focused on vocabulary produced moderate effects in these areas. Second, instruction that is carefully designed and delivered can significantly increase the early literacy skills of kindergarten children at risk of reading failure. With specific regard to vocabulary, these results imply that (a) vocabulary development should be an important focus of early literacy intervention, and (b) explicitly teaching word meanings within the context of shared storybook reading is an effective method for increasing the vocabulary of young children at risk of experiencing reading difficulties.

Although these results support the overall effectiveness of the storybook intervention, we were interested in whether some students may have responded differentially. Previous research has indicated that children with lower initial vocabularies learn fewer word meanings during traditional storybook reading activities than children with higher vocabularies (Nicholson & Whyte, 1992; Penno et al., 2002; Robbins & Ehri, 1994). In the next section, we present secondary analyses of the data from this study that examine whether there were differential effects of the storybook intervention for students who began kindergarten with low receptive vocabulary skills.

METHOD

Participants

To examine whether there were differential effects of the storybook intervention for students with low receptive vocabulary, we conducted secondary analyses on data from the same kindergarten students that participated in the larger study. Students were selected to participate in the intervention study because they were considered to be at risk based on their performance on letter naming and phonological awareness tasks. However, these students also demonstrated below-average receptive vocabulary. The average standard score on the Peabody Picture Vocabulary Test (PPVT; Dunn & Dunn, 1981) was 92, meaning that the receptive vocabulary of the "average" participant in the study was at the 30th percentile compared to a nationally normed sample.

For purposes of these analyses, we looked at student data from two of the three intervention groups, the group that received the storybook intervention ($n = 34$) and the control group ($n = 30$) that received a sounds and letters module of a commercial reading program (Open Court; Adams et al., 2000). We chose to focus our analyses on these two groups to provide a clearer comparison between students who received the storybook intervention and students in the control group. Previous analyses indicated that there were no differences between the control group and the code-based group on

TABLE 3
Means and Standard Deviations of Vocabulary Pretest
and Posttest Measures by Group

| | Pretest | | | | | | Posttest | | | | | |
| | Storybook | | | Control | | | Storybook | | | Control | | |
Measure	M	SD	n	M	SD	n	M	SD	n	M	SD	n
PPVT	92.03	13.12	37	91.87	12.34	37	—	—	—	—	—	—
Taught vocabulary	9.36	5.12	33	11.25	5.11	28	15.38	5.54	34	11.80	4.83	30
Untaught vocabulary	8.03	3.55	32	8.27	4.26	30	11.79	4.89	34	10.77	4.99	30

Note.   PPVT = Peabody Picture Vocabulary Test.

vocabulary outcomes. Descriptive statistics for participants on measures of vocabulary are displayed in Table 3. The sample sizes at each testing period vary slightly due to attrition and missing data. Information on sample sizes at each measurement point are included in the table.

Measure of Vocabulary Growth

At pre- and posttest, all participants were administered a measure assessing selected vocabulary from the stories used in storybook intervention. The National Reading Panel (2000) concluded that specific vocabulary growth is best assessed through researcher-developed measures because these measures are more sensitive to gains achieved through instruction than are standardized tools. To assess specific vocabulary growth, we developed a 20-word instrument in which students were asked to produce word meanings or tell anything they knew about target words. Ten specific words were randomly selected from the pool of explicitly taught vocabulary, and the remaining 10 words were randomly selected from the pool of words that appeared in the stories but received no explicit instructional emphasis. No more than one word per story occurred in the measure.

The measure was individually administered at pre- and postintervention in two separate sessions of 10 words each. Each assessment item consisted of two questions: (a) asking the definition of the word (e.g., "What is a principal?" "What does roared mean?"), and (b) asking a what, when, or how question (e.g., "What does a principal do?" "What do you do when you roar?"). To guide scoring, definitions for each word were specified, including dictionary definitions, synonyms, and the informal definition used during storybook instruction. A panel of four scorers further determined the criteria, awarding points to responses that did not match the listed definitions or synonyms. Student responses were scored on a scale of 0 to 3 points per word. A score of 3 was awarded to responses matching the listed definitions or synonyms; responses that had no relation to the listed definitions received 0 points. A separate total score was calculated for each student for taught words and untaught words. Total possible scores on each of the assessments ranged from 0 to 30 points. Interscorer reliability calculated on 10% of the words was above 90%.

RESULTS

To test models of differential effectiveness based on students' initial receptive vocabulary, we compared the regressions of vocabulary posttest measures (taught and untaught)
on pretest levels of the same variables and the pretest level of PPVT. Because we were interested in comparing vocabulary growth both across groups (i.e., the storybook group
compared with the control group) and within groups (i.e., taught vocabulary compared
with untaught vocabulary within the storybook group), we used structural equation modeling (SEM) to estimate a bivariate outcome regression model. The fact that the taught
and untaught outcomes were substantially correlated and likely to remain so even after
controlling for predictors precluded the use of simpler ordinary least squares regression
procedures.

To address group equivalency at pretest, we employed random assignment of participant to condition and also constrained the pretest parameters (means, standard deviations, and correlations) to be equal across the groups. Estimation was carried out
using M-Plus (Muthén & Muthén, 1998) using full information maximum likelihood
assuming missing data were missing at random, that is, missing at random conditional
on predictors included in the model. We constructed linear combinations of model parameters and standard errors to obtain critical ratios to examine differential effectiveness. Because of the modest sample size, we referred our critical ratios to the t distri-
bution with degrees of freedom equal to the total sample size minus the number of
fixed effects for obtaining p values.

Figure 1 shows a path diagram of the bivariate outcome regression model. Observed
variables are shown by squares, latent variables by circles. Single-headed arrows starting
from the predictor and going to the outcome indicate regression paths. Covariances or
correlations are shown as double-headed arrows. An uppercase I indicates a regression
intercept. Parameter estimates are shown as numbers in the diagram next to, or on, the
model parameters they reference (e.g., the numbers on the single-headed arrows are the
parameter estimates for the regression paths). All values attached to double-headed arrows are correlations, and the values next to the latent residual error variables (e_1 and e_2)
are residual standard deviations. Estimates for the control group are shown above, and
the corresponding estimates for the storybook group are shown below. The chi-square
statistic at the bottom is based on the degrees of freedom created by the constraints on the
pretest parameters. As can be seen in Figure 1, the constraints do not cause a significant
decrement in fit.

All the pretest measures were centered about their respective grand means across
groups so that the regression intercepts at the posttest represent the mean difference on
the outcomes for children at mean levels of the pretest measures. As was the case in the
primary analyses (Simmons et al., 2004), this model reveals an overall effect for group
on taught vocabulary, $t(64) = 3.70, p < .001$, but not for untaught vocabulary, $t(64) = 1.30$,
$p = .20$. In other words, students in the storybook group learned and demonstrated greater
knowledge of target vocabulary than students in the control condition, but there were no
group differences on untaught vocabulary.

Figure 2 uses the observed data to illustrate graphically the regressions of the
residualized outcome scores plotted against the residualized initial PPVT scores for

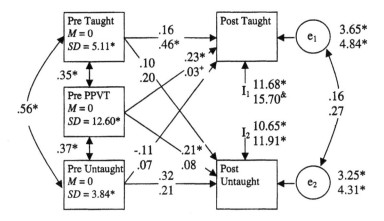

Chi-Square = 8.60, df = 9, p = .48, RMSEA = .00

FIGURE 1   Path diagram of structural equation modeling of differential effectiveness. Control group parameters are on top, corresponding intervention group parameters are below except where constrained to be equal at the pretest. *Indicates the parameter is significantly different from zero. +Indicates the parameter is not significantly different from zero but is significantly different from the corresponding parameter in the other group. &Indicates the parameter is significantly different from zero and significantly different from the corresponding parameter in the other group. Pretest means were centered to zero to make regression intercepts more interpretable. PPVT = Peabody Picture Vocabulary Test.

taught and untaught vocabulary separately by group. This allows a visual examination of the fitted regression slopes for taught and untaught vocabulary for both the storybook and control groups. Because these simple regressions do not take into account missing data and the correlation between the two outcomes at posttest, the statistics are slightly different than those produced by the SEM model. The overall pattern of results, however, is the same. The intervention group is labeled "Storybook" and the control group is labeled "Open Court." Basic regression statistics are shown across the top margin of each plot.

Differential Effects Across Groups

To examine differential effects across groups, we examined t statistics testing whether the effects of initial PPVT were significantly different for students in the storybook group compared to students in the control group. For example, if the storybook intervention was uniformly beneficial regardless of initial status on PPVT, the effects would be the same across the two groups. Likewise, the slopes of the regression lines in Figure 2 would appear similar in both the storybook and control groups. On the other hand, if the storybook intervention tended to benefit students with initial high PPVT scores the most, the effect would be greater in the storybook group. In this case, the regression line would be steeper in the storybook group than in the control group. Finally, if the storybook intervention had a compensatory effect, students with initially lower PPVT scores would benefit the most compared to the control group, the effect

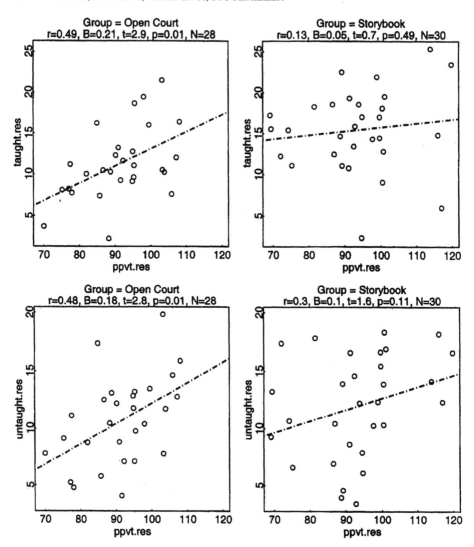

FIGURE 2   Residualized initial Peabody Picture Vocabulary Test (PPVT) scores versus residualized outcome scores for taught and untaught vocabulary.

would be greater in the control group, and the regressions would appear flatter in the storybook group than the control group.

According to the SEM analyses, there was a statistically significant difference in the effect of initial PPVT for taught vocabulary between the storybook group and the control group, $t(61) = 2.07$, $p = .04$. In Figure 2, the slope of the regression line for taught vocabulary in the storybook group is clearly flatter than the slope of the regression line for the control group. Conversely, there was not a statistically significant difference in the effect of initial PPVT for untaught vocabulary between the storybook group and the control group, $t(64) = 1.45$, $p = .15$. In this case, although the slope of the regression line for untaught vocabulary in the storybook group appears to be slightly flatter than the slope of the regression line for the control group, this difference is noticeably smaller than for taught vocabulary and is not statistically significant.

For taught vocabulary, this finding indicates that in comparison with students in the control group, the storybook intervention was differentially effective based on initial PPVT scores. This result clarifies the main effect finding that students who received the storybook intervention made greater gains in taught vocabulary than students in a control group. Specifically, the finding of differential effectiveness suggests that students with lower receptive vocabulary benefited more from the storybook intervention in relation to students who did not receive the storybook intervention.

For untaught vocabulary, primary analyses revealed that there was no main effect of group. In other words, students in the storybook group did not learn the meanings of untaught words at a greater rate than students in the control group. This result is reinforced by the finding showing no differential effects based on initial vocabulary status. Although there is a slight trend suggesting that students with lower initial PPVT scores may have benefited more, this result was not statistically significant.

Differential Effects Within Groups

To examine differential effects within groups, we examined t statistics testing whether the effects of initial PPVT were significantly different than zero for taught and untaught vocabulary in the storybook and control groups separately. If the effect was significantly greater than zero, this would indicate that students with higher initial PPVT scores made greater vocabulary gains between pretest and posttest than students with lower initial PPVT scores. If the effect was not significantly different than zero, this would indicate that all students made similar vocabulary gains, regardless of initial PPVT scores.

According to the bivariate SEM model, the PPVT effects on both taught and untaught vocabulary in the control group were significantly greater than zero; respectively, $t(64) = 3.20, p < .01$, and $t(64) = 3.33, p < .01$. In addition, the effects for taught and untaught vocabulary were not significantly different from each other, $t(64) = 0.19$, $p = .85$. In fact, the coefficients were almost identical. These results indicate that in the control group, students with higher initial PPVT scores made greater gains on both taught and untaught vocabulary than students with lower initial PPVT scores. This can be seen in Figure 2 in the very similar positive slopes for the Open Court group on both taught and untaught vocabulary.

According to the bivariate SEM model, the PPVT effects on both taught and untaught vocabulary in the storybook group were not significantly greater than zero; respectively, $t(64) = 0.37, p = .71$, and $t(64) = 1.42, p = .16$. Similar to the control group, the effects for taught and untaught vocabulary in the storybook group were not significantly different from each other, $t(64) = 0.83, p = .21$. These results indicate that in the storybook group, all students made similar gains irrespective of initial PPVT scores. These results are also visually apparent in Figure 2 where the regression slopes appear much flatter. However, unlike the control group in which the slopes appear almost indistinguishable, the slope for taught vocabulary is noticeably flatter than the slope for untaught vocabulary, although this difference is not statistically significant.

DISCUSSION

We developed our experimental storybook intervention with the goal of decreasing the vocabulary gap among kindergarten students who were at risk of experiencing reading difficulties. Because previous research suggests that traditional storybook reading activities tend to reinforce and widen this gap (Penno et al., 2002; Robbins & Ehri, 1994), we intensified our intervention by explicitly teaching the meanings of specific words in the stories. The purpose of this study was to conduct analyses investigating whether the intensified storybook intervention produced differential effects on measures of vocabulary taught explicitly in the intervention as well as vocabulary in the stories but not targeted directly for instruction.

Primary analyses from our intervention study revealed that students who received the storybook intervention made greater growth than a control group on an experimenter-developed measure of explicitly taught vocabulary (Simmons et al., 2004). Unlike studies evaluating traditional storybook reading activities, results of secondary analyses indicated no evidence of a differential effect favoring students with larger vocabularies. In fact, for words that were taught explicitly in the storybook intervention, we found the opposite effect. Using SEM procedures, we found a statistically significant difference in the effect of initial PPVT scores on taught vocabulary outcomes between the storybook group and the control group. This result is reinforced visually by the clear positive regression slope for taught vocabulary in the control group compared with the nearly flat slope in the storybook group. These findings suggest that students with lower receptive vocabulary skills demonstrated greater gains in taught vocabulary than students with higher receptive vocabulary in comparison to students in the control group.

Conversely, our primary analyses indicated that, overall, students in the storybook intervention did not demonstrate greater growth on untaught vocabulary than students in the control group (Simmons et al., 2004). These findings are inconsistent with the results of previous research suggesting that students do learn the meanings of unknown words through incidental exposure during storybook reading activities (Elley, 1989; Nicholson & Whyte, 1992; Robbins & Ehri, 1994; Senechal & Cornell, 1993).

One possible explanation for these findings is related to the manner in which we measured vocabulary growth. Other studies have typically measured vocabulary growth immediately after exposing students to new words in the context of relatively short storybook reading interventions (i.e., 1–3 weeks). In our study, we measured vocabulary growth in May after a 7-month intervention in which some of the words assessed at posttest had not been read in storybooks for many months. Our measure, therefore, was more similar to a delayed maintenance test rather than a test of immediate effects. Although this made our measure less sensitive to immediate gains, it did make it a more stringent measure of long-term vocabulary growth. Consequently, our results do not indicate whether students learned the meanings of untaught words when they were first read in the stories, only that any differences between groups had disappeared by the posttest.

Secondary analyses reinforced these primary findings by indicating that there were no differential effects qualifying the main effect. The lack of a statistically significant difference in the effect of initial PPVT scores for untaught vocabulary between the storybook group and the control group indicated that students with both higher and lower initial

PPVT scores demonstrated the same growth as students in the control group. This finding can be clarified by examining the pattern of growth demonstrated by students in the control group. Because these students were not intentionally exposed to any of the vocabulary in the stories, any growth should be explained by typical development. The statistically significant positive effect of initial PPVT scores on both outcomes suggests that students with higher vocabularies learned new word meanings at a greater rate than students with lower vocabularies. This conclusion is consistent with research on vocabulary development, especially for students in the early grades (Biemiller & Slonim, 2001; Stanovich, 1986). Apparently then, students in the storybook group learned the meanings of words in the stories, but not words directly targeted for instruction, at a rate similar to what would be expected as the result of typical development. If typical development can be characterized by a gradual increase in the gap between students with higher and lower vocabularies, then the intervention did nothing to counteract this trend.

In summary, the goal of vocabulary interventions for young children at risk of experiencing reading difficulties is to narrow, or at least intercept the widening vocabulary gap among students. To accomplish this goal, interventions must result in comparable or greater word learning for students with smaller initial vocabularies than for students with larger vocabularies. Previous research has demonstrated that listening to storybooks is an effective way to increase students' vocabularies (National Reading Panel, 2000). The results of our analyses, however, suggest that storybook reading activities that rely on incidental exposure to unknown words do nothing to decrease the vocabulary gap.

On the other hand, our analyses indicated that teaching word meanings explicitly within the context of storybook readings resulted in the same amount of vocabulary growth for students with smaller initial vocabularies as for students with larger vocabularies. In addition, the storybook intervention was differentially more effective for students with smaller vocabularies compared to the control group. In other words, direct teaching of vocabulary did not act to widen the vocabulary gap but instead helped to diminish it.

IMPLICATIONS FOR INSTRUCTION

The findings of this study hold promise for improving early intervention efforts for young children at risk of reading difficulties with less developed vocabularies. By intensifying shared book reading activities with direct teaching of specific word meanings, interventions can increase students' knowledge of target vocabulary (see also Wasik & Bond, 2001). Explicit vocabulary instruction that intentionally draws attention to target words within the context of storybooks may also help young students develop a greater overall awareness of words and word meanings. This enhanced word consciousness may then increase the likelihood that students will learn the meanings of unknown words independently and incidentally by attending more closely to words and their use (Baumann et al., 2003).

Despite these positive findings, there remain many critical issues regarding how to accelerate vocabulary growth among children who enter with meaningful differences. Specifically, when time is limited and the differences between entry-level skills of students are great, how do we optimally alter learning trajectories? In domains such as phonemic awareness and alphabetic understanding, there is general agreement about what to teach and how to teach (National Reading Panel, 2000). In vocabulary, however, there is less empirical evidence to guide our efforts. The current study adds to the literature on how to teach by incorporating principles of explicit vocabulary instruction (e.g., Beck et al., 2002) within storybook reading activities (e.g., Whitehurst et al., 1999).

Yet, the issue of what to teach, or the critical vocabulary that matters most, continues to remain elusive. Although effective interventions can begin to close the vocabulary gap, direct teaching of individual word meanings is extremely time intensive, there is a limited number of words that can be taught explicitly, and the rate of typical vocabulary development is steep. Therefore, to optimize scarce instructional time, it is crucial to teach words that will have the most impact and leverage in decreasing the vocabulary gap. Researchers are beginning to provide some guidance on the critical vocabulary or what to teach (Biemiller, 2003; Biemiller & Slonim, 2001). However, until we have a better understanding of which words to teach deeply, intentionally, and explicitly, closing the vocabulary gap will remain a persistent and consistent challenge.

ACKNOWLEDGMENTS

Preparation of this article was supported in part by Project Optimize Grant H324C980156, Office of Special Education Programs, U.S. Department of Education. This material does not necessarily represent the policy of the U.S. Department of Education, nor is the material necessarily endorsed by the Federal Government.

REFERENCES

Adams, M. J., Bereiter, C., Brown, A., Campione, J., Carruthers, I., Case, R., et al. (2000). *Open court reading.* Columbus, OH: SRA.

Anderson, R. C., & Nagy, W. E. (1992). The vocabulary conundrum. *American Educator, 16*(4), 14–18, 44–47.

Baker, S. K., Simmons, D. C., & Kame'enui, E. J. (1998). Vocabulary acquisition: Research bases. In D. C. Simmons & E. J. Kame'enui (Eds.), *What reading research tells us about children with diverse learning needs* (pp. 183–218). Mahwah, NJ: Lawrence Erlbaum Associates, Inc.

Baumann, J. F., Kame'enui, E. J., & Ash, G. E. (2003). Research on vocabulary instruction: Voltaire redux. In J. Flood, J. Jensen, D. Lapp, & J. R. Squire (Eds.), *Handbook of research on teaching the English language arts* (pp. 752–785). New York: Macmillan.

Beck, I. L., McKeown, M. G., & Kucan, L. (2002). *Bringing words to life: Robust vocabulary instruction.* New York: Guilford.

Beck, I. L., Perfetti, C. A., & McKeown, M. G. (1982). Effects of long-term vocabulary instruction on lexical access and reading comprehension. *Journal of Educational Psychology, 74,* 506–521.

Becker, W. C. (1977). Teaching reading and language to the disadvantaged: What we have learned from field research. *Harvard Educational Review, 47,* 518–543.

Biemiller, A. (2001). Teaching vocabulary: Early, direct, and sequential. *American Educator, 25*(1), 24–28, 47.

Biemiller, A. (2003). Teaching vocabulary in the primary grades: Vocabulary instruction needed. In J. F. Baumann & E. J. Kame'enui (Eds.), *Vocabulary instruction: Research to practice* (pp. 28–40). New York: Guilford.

Biemiller, A., & Slonim, N. (2001). Estimating root word vocabulary growth in normative and advantaged populations: Evidence for a common sequence of vocabulary acquisition. *Journal of Educational Psychology, 93,* 498–520.

Bus, A. G., van Ijzendoorn, M. H., & Pelegrina, A. D. (1995). Joint book reading makes for success in learning to read: A meta-analysis on intergenerational transmission of literacy. *Review of Educational Research, 65,* 1–21.

Coyne, M. D., Kame'enui, E. J., & Simmons, D. C. (2001). Prevention and intervention in beginning reading: Two complex systems. *Learning Disabilities Research & Practice, 16,* 62–72.

Cunningham, A. E., & Stanovich, K. E. (1998). What reading does for the mind. *American Educator, 22*(1–2), 8–15.

Dickinson, D. K., & Smith, M. W. (1994). Long-term effects of preschool teachers' book readings on low-income children's vocabulary and story comprehension. *Reading Research Quarterly, 29,* 104–122.

Dunn, L., & Dunn, L. (1981). *Peabody Picture Vocabulary Test–Revised.* Circle Pines, MN: American Guidance Service.

Elley, W. B. (1989). Vocabulary acquisition from listening to stories. *Reading Research Quarterly, 24,* 174–187.

Foorman, B. R., Francis, D. J., Fletcher, J. M., Schatschneider, C., & Mehta, P. (1998). The role of instruction in learning to read: Preventing reading failure in at-risk children. *Journal of Educational Psychology, 90,* 37–55.

Foorman, B. R., & Torgesen, J. (2001). Critical elements of classroom and small-group instruction promote reading success in all children. *Learning Disabilities Research & Practice, 16,* 203–212.

Good, R. H., III, Simmons, D. C., & Kame'enui, E. J. (2001). The importance of decision-making utility of a continuum of fluency-based indicators of foundational reading skills for third-grade high-stakes outcomes. *Scientific Studies of Reading, 5,* 257–288.

Hart, B., & Risley, R. T. (1995). *Meaningful differences in the everyday experience of young American children.* Baltimore: Brookes.

Hayes, D. P., & Ahrens, M. (1988). Vocabulary simplification for children: A special case of "motherese." *Journal of Child Language, 15,* 395–410.

Kame'enui, E. J., Carnine, D. W., Dixon, R. C., Simmons, D. C., & Coyne, M. D. (2002). *Effective teaching strategies that accommodate diverse learners* (2nd ed.). Columbus, OH: Merrill.

Kame'enui, E., Carnine, D., & Freschi, R. (1982). Effects of text construction and instructional procedures for teaching word meanings on comprehension and recall. *Reading Research Quarterly, 17,* 367–388.

McKeown, M. G., & Beck, I. L. (2003). Direct and rich vocabulary instruction. In J. F. Baumann & E. J. Kame'enui (Eds.), *Vocabulary instruction: Research to practice* (pp. 13–27). New York: Guilford.

McKeown, M. G., Beck, I. L., Omanson, R. C., & Perfetti, C. A. (1983). The effects of long-term vocabulary instruction on reading comprehension: A replication. *Journal of Reading Behavior, 15,* 3–18.

Muthén, B., & Muthén, L. (1998). *Mplus user's guide.* Los Angeles: Author.

National Reading Panel. (2000). *Teaching children to read: An evidence-based assessment of the scientific research literature on reading and its implications for reading instruction: Reports of the subgroups.* Bethesda, MD: National Institute of Child Health and Human Development.

National Research Council. (1998). *Preventing reading difficulties in young children.* Washington, DC: National Academy Press.

Nicholson, T., & Whyte, B. (1992). Matthew effects in learning new words while listening to stories. In C. K. Kinzer & D. J. Leu (Eds.), *Literacy research, theory, and practice: Views from many perspectives: Forty-First Yearbook of the National Reading Conference* (pp. 499–503). Chicago: National Reading Conference.

No Child Left Behind. (2002). United States Department of Education. Retrieved April 7, 2002, from http://www.nclb.gov/index.html

Penno, J. F., Wilkinson, I. A. G., & Moore, D. W. (2002). Vocabulary acquisition from teacher explanation and repeated listening to stories: Do they overcome the Matthew effect? *Journal of Educational Psychology, 94,* 23–33.

Robbins, C., & Ehri, L. C. (1994). Reading storybooks to kindergartners helps them learn new vocabulary words. *Journal of Educational Psychology, 86,* 54–64.

Senechal, M. (1997). The differential effect of storybook reading on preschoolers' acquisition of expressive and receptive vocabulary. *Journal of Child Language, 24,* 123–138.

Senechal, M., & Cornell, E. H. (1993). Vocabulary acquisition through shared reading experiences. *Reading Research Quarterly, 28,* 360–374.

Senechal, M., Thomas, E., & Monker, J. (1995). Individual differences in 4-year-old children's acquisition of vocabulary during storybook reading. *Journal of Educational Psychology, 87,* 218–229.

Simmons, D. C., Kame'enui, E. J., Harn, B. A., Edwards, L. A., Coyne, M. D., Thomas-Beck, C., et al. (2004). *The effects of instructional emphasis and specificity on early reading and vocabulary development of kindergarten children.* Manuscript submitted for publication.

Simmons, D. C., Kame'enui, E. J., Stoolmiller, M., Coyne, M. D., & Harn, B. A. (2003). Accelerating growth and maintaining proficiency: A two-year intervention study of kindergarten and first-grade children at risk for reading difficulties. In B. Foorman (Ed.), *Preventing and remediating reading difficulties: Bringing science to scale* (pp. 197–228). Timonium, MD: York Press.

Snow, C. E. (1991). The theoretical basis for relationships between language and literacy in development. *Journal of Research in Childhood Education, 6,* 5–10.

Stahl, S. A. (1986). Three principles of effective vocabulary instruction. *Journal of Reading, 29,* 662–668.

Stahl, S. A., & Fairbanks, M. M. (1986). The effects of vocabulary instruction: A model-based meta-analysis. *Review of Educational Research, 56,* 72–110.

Stahl, S. A., & Shiel, T. G. (1999). Teaching meaning vocabulary: Productive approaches for poor readers. In *Read all about it! Readings to inform the profession* (pp. 291–321). Sacramento: California State Board of Education.

Stanovich, K. E. (1986). Matthew effects in reading: Some consequences of individual differences in the acquisition of literacy. *Reading Research Quarterly, 21,* 360–406.

Storch, S. A., & Whitehurst, G. J. (2002). Oral language and code-related precursors to reading: Evidence from a longitudinal structural model. *Developmental Psychology, 38,* 934–947.

Torgesen, J. K. (2000). Individual differences in response to early interventions in reading: The lingering problem of treatment resisters. *Learning Disabilities Research & Practice, 15,* 55–64.

Torgesen, J. K., Wagner, R. K., Rashotte, C. A., Rose, E., Lindamood, P., Conway, T., et al. (1999). Preventing reading failure in young children with phonological processing disabilities: Group and individual responses to instruction. *Journal of Educational Psychology, 91,* 1–15.

Wasik, B. A., & Bond, M. A. (2001). Beyond the pages of a book: Interactive book reading and language development in preschool classrooms. *Journal of Educational Psychology, 93,* 243–250.

Whitehurst, G. J., Arnold, D. H., Epstein, J. N., Angell, A. L., Smith, M., & Fischel, J. E. (1994). A picture book reading intervention in day care and home for children from low-income families. *Developmental Psychology, 30,* 679–689.

Whitehurst, G. J., Epstein, J. N., Angell, A. L., Payne, A. C., Crone, D. A., & Fischel, J. E. (1994). Outcomes of an emergent literacy intervention in Head Start. *Journal of Educational Psychology, 86,* 542–555.

Whitehurst, G. J., Zevenbergen, A. A., Crone, D. A., Schultz, M. D., Velting, O. N., & Fischel, J. E. (1999). Outcomes of an emergent literacy intervention from Head Start through second grade. *Journal of Educational Psychology, 91,* 261–272.

The Promise and Limitations
of Reading Instruction in the Mainstream:
The Need for a Multilevel Approach

Eric Dion
Department of Special Education and Vocational Training
Université du Québec à Montréal

Paul L. Morgan, Douglas Fuchs, and Lynn S. Fuchs
Department of Special Education
Peabody College, Vanderbilt University

The purpose of this article is to describe how increasingly intensive, multilevel interventions can be used to ensure the increase in number of children who learn to read. We first review the promise and limitations of empirically validated best practices for mainstream classrooms. We then discuss results from a recent multilevel intervention study. We conclude by examining implications of a multilevel instructional approach for special education service delivery.

We have all witnessed how much some children struggle with reading. Consider the case of Josh. He is in third grade but is reading at a level more akin to a first grader. He reads slowly and painfully. He makes many mistakes, often trying to guess the words. He does not grasp much of the text content and, perhaps unsurprisingly, shows a complete lack of interest in books. As a matter of fact, he tries more and more to avoid reading altogether, which, of course, will only slow his development as a reader (see Cunningham & Stanovich, 1998). Unfortunately, Josh is not an isolated case. Up to 40% of children struggle to become proficient readers, an indication that many are unable to benefit from typical classroom instruction (Snow, Burns, & Griffin, 1998). Given the plight of Josh and so many others like him, can teachers do anything to ensure that all children learn to read?

A growing body of work suggests that the answer to this question is a hopeful but qualified yes. That is, there is both promise and limitations in what we can currently offer

Requests for reprints should be sent to Eric Dion, Département d'éducation et formation spécialisées, Université du Québec à Montréal, C.P. 8888, Succursale Centre-ville, Montréal, Québec, Canada H3C 3P8. E-mail: dion.e@uqam.edu children like Josh. The purpose of this article is to examine outcomes of empirically validated best practices with an emphasis on the First-Grade Peer Assisted Learning Strategies (PALS) Reading Program (D. Fuchs, Fuchs, Thompson, Svenson, et al., 2001; D. Fuchs, Fuchs, Yen, et al., 2001; Mathes, Howard, Allen, & Fuchs, 1998). Research on the nature of difficulties encountered by struggling readers is first described as well as components of effective instruction for these children. The general effectiveness of PALS and other best practices is then briefly reviewed. We argue that despite its effectiveness with most children, no best practice in reading instruction is universally effective; a significant proportion of children, aptly termed *nonresponders,* fail to make adequate progress. We present results from a recent experimental study in which increasingly individualized and intensive interventions were offered to nonresponders to boost their reading achievement. We conclude with an analysis of the implications for serving nonresponders through special education.

COMPONENTS OF EFFECTIVE READING INSTRUCTION

There is growing consensus on core skills necessary to become a proficient reader (e.g., Adams, 1990; National Institute of Child Health and Human Development, 2000; Pressley, 2002; Snow et al., 1998). These skills include phonological awareness, decoding, reading fluency, an adequate vocabulary, and reading comprehension (National Institute of Child Health and Human Development, 2000). One skill in particular, phonological awareness, seems to act as a major bottleneck for some children (Adams, 1990).

This consensus about requisite skills is based on two broad sets of research findings. First, longitudinal studies indicate that children who fail to acquire the more elementary core skills soon after entering school become, by and large, poor readers. Juel (1988), for example, found that children completing first grade with poor phonemic awareness were likely to remain poor readers in fourth grade (with a probability of almost .90). Francis, Shaywitz, Stuebing, Shaywitz, and Fletcher (1996) found that 74% of third-grade struggling readers remained poor readers in ninth grade. This longitudinal work indicates that most poor readers do not "catch up" unless they receive an early and effective remediation.

Second, many experimental studies indicate that poor readers who are provided explicit instruction in the core skills often become better readers. This holds true when these children are provided phonological awareness training (O'Connor, Notari-Syverson, & Vadasy, 1996, 1998; Rashotte, MacPhee, & Torgesen, 2001; Torgesen & Davis, 1996; Torgesen et al., 1999; Uhry & Shepherd, 1997; Vellutino et al., 1996), explicit phonics instruction (Rashotte et al., 2001; Torgesen et al., 1999), and increased opportunities to read text (Hatcher, Hulme, & Ellis, 1994; Rashotte et al., 2001; Torgesen et al., 1999; Vellutino et al., 1996). For example, Torgesen et al. randomly assigned 180 kindergartners identified as poor readers to a control group or to one of three different experimental conditions, including a phonological awareness plus synthetic phonics (PASP) intervention. The PASP group received one-to-one tutoring focused on building phonological awareness and applying it to decoding individual words. Tutoring was provided outside the classroom by a trained specialist. At the end of the intervention, children in the PASP group outperformed controls on measures of phonological awareness, phonemic decoding, and untimed word reading, although between-group differences in reading comprehension were not statistically significant.

Results from longitudinal and experimental studies strongly argue for providing skills instruction earlier rather than later. Indeed, developing the core skills quickly is so important that children who enter first or second grade without them are often considered at risk both for continued reading failure and for many undesirable long-range outcomes. A child who still displays severe reading deficits by third grade, for example, is far less likely to graduate from high school or find employment (Snow et al., 1998) and is far more likely to be adjudicated, incarcerated, and poor (Adams, 1990; Smith, 1998).

The aforementioned research efforts, and many others not mentioned here, permit fairly accurate predictions about which children will struggle to become competent readers. This research also provides practitioners with empirically validated, generally effective interventions to alleviate the difficulties of these readers. How then do we transfer this expertise to the classroom? A limitation of many intervention studies is that they rely on one-to-one tutoring provided by a trained specialist outside the classroom. Torgesen et al. (1999), for example, provided up to 88 hr of individualized instruction to their sample of poor readers. At best, the typical school has resources to offer out-of-classroom one-to-one tutoring to only a very small number of children. It is also probably unrealistic to presume that regular classroom teachers are able to offer to struggling readers the individualized attention they apparently need.

What is needed, clearly, are classwide, cost-efficient, and teacher-friendly programs that can benefit a large number of struggling readers as early as possible. A number of programs meeting these criteria have been developed over the years (e.g., Foorman, Francis, Fletcher, Schatschneider, & Mehta, 1998; Greenwood, Delquadri, & Hall, 1989; Rosenshine & Meister, 1994). We focus here on the First-Grade PALS Reading Program. In PALS, first graders of different ability levels are paired to work together to practice and master skills such as phonological awareness, letter–sound correspondence, decoding, sight–word recognition, and fluent text reading. These activities are structured so that there is role reciprocity (Simmons, Fuchs, Fuchs, Hodge, & Mathes, 1994) and frequent verbal interactions and feedback between the stronger and weaker readers, with many opportunities to respond (Greenwood et al., 1989). PALS lessons are typically conducted three times a week, with each session lasting about 35 min.

PALS works well in mainstream classrooms. Its activities improve the reading fluency and comprehension skills of high-, average-, and low-achieving students and students with disabilities compared to controls of similar reading ability (e.g., D. Fuchs, Fuchs, Mathes, & Simmons, 1997; D. Fuchs, Fuchs, Thompson, Al Otaiba, et al., 2001; Mathes et al., 1998). In one study of first-grade students (D. Fuchs, Fuchs, Yen, et al., 2001), PALS students outperformed controls by about .50 standard deviations on both phonological awareness and alphabetic measures (i.e., measures involving spelling and reading both nonsense and real words). Students in PALS classrooms who played a short fluency-building game across 20 weeks outperformed controls on fluency and comprehension measures by .20 to .30 standard deviations. Moreover, these results were not mediated by type of student (i.e., students with disabilities vs. low achievers vs. average achievers vs. high achievers). Thus, PALS led to improved reading by both young children at risk and those already identified as disabled. These findings conform with a best evidence synthesis of studies assessing peer tutoring in reading with students with disabilities. The average effect size based on 11 studies was .36, with effect sizes ranging from .07 to .75 (Mathes & Fuchs, 1994).

STUDENTS UNRESPONSIVE TO READING INSTRUCTION

Whereas the results of reading intervention research are encouraging, there is a persisting problem: Not all children respond to even our best current methods, including intensive one-to-one tutoring. Vellutino et al.'s (1996) intervention study is a telling example. Vellutino et al. implemented a prevention program to boost the skills of poor readers with normal IQs. The children received 30 min of daily one-to-one tutoring for a minimum of 15 weeks to a maximum of 25 weeks (i.e., 35–65 hr of intervention). A variety of strategies for word identification was explicitly taught, including phonetic decoding and sight–word recognition. Most children also read from connected text. Their rate of word reading was evaluated during first and second grade. Although most children benefited from the intervention, 25% showed limited progress, still performing below the 30th percentile on reading measures by the end of second grade. In short, these children did not become proficient readers, even after the provision of a well-planned and costly intervention delivered in a research (i.e., quality controlled) context.

There are at least three reasons why it is important to know more about these nonreaders, or nonresponders. First, increased understanding will help to design programs that better meet their needs. Second, it will facilitate the study of these children's cognitive and language-processing characteristics and may help distinguish truly disabled readers (i.e., those not responding to effective intervention) from children who simply did not receive adequate reading instruction (Clay, 1987; Vellutino et al., 1996). Third, nonresponsiveness is increasingly proposed as an alternative to IQ–achievement discrepancy as the primary diagnostic criterion for learning disabilities (see D. Fuchs, Mock, Morgan, & Young, 2003). Further study of nonresponders is required to empirically substantiate this approach.

Current interest in nonresponders notwithstanding, there is still considerable uncertainty and controversy regarding what constitutes nonresponsiveness. Torgesen (2000) suggested that nonresponders are children below the 30th percentile on reading measures at the end of a generally effective intervention. Yet, individual differences in reading achievement are unavoidable, and even if effective programs become commonplace, 30% of the children must by definition fall below the 30th percentile in any validation sample. Good, Kaminsky, and Shinn (1999) recommended instead an absolute performance standard, suggesting, for instance, that by the end of first grade, students who read below 40 words correctly per minute are seriously deficient in reading. Although an absolute criterion for identifying nonresponders may represent an improvement over a relative one, basing identification solely on performance level (i.e., reading achievement at the end of intervention) is insufficient.

Conceptually, nonresponsiveness implies both a low performance level and an inadequate learning rate in the context of what is generally an effective intervention. Thus, there is a need for a dual-discrepancy criterion. Consider an example from pediatric medicine (see L. S. Fuchs, Fuchs, & Speece, 2002). When monitoring a child's physical growth, the endocrinologist is interested in the quality of the child's environment, her height at a given point in time (i.e., performance level), and her growth velocity over time (i.e., learning rate). The hypothesis of an underlying pathology for a child who is small relative to same-age peers is seriously considered only if the environment is appropriately nurturing and the child's growth trajectory is flatter than that of appropriate comparison groups. If this last condition is not met, the child is considered to be benefiting from or responding to her environment, and no special intervention with its associated risks is undertaken. This is the rationale on which the dual-discrepancy criterion is based (Al Otaiba & Fuchs, 2002; L. S. Fuchs & Fuchs, 1998; L. S. Fuchs et al., 2002; Speece & Case, 2001). It carries two implications. First, if despite a relatively poor performance level, struggling readers are progressing at a rate commensurate with the growth rates of other children exposed to the same instructional environment, they are responding: They may be achieving commensurate with their learning capacity and benefiting from instruction. No special intervention is warranted. Second, if all the children, including suspected nonresponders, are demonstrating little or no growth, the adequacy of classroom instruction must be questioned before any student can be identified as unresponsive.

The dual discrepancy requires measurement sensitive to individual change; nonresponsiveness is a student characteristic that must be determined with confidence. Curriculum-based measurement (CBM) is one such measurement system (Deno, 1985). The educational relevance, psychometric soundness, and sensitivity to change of this method has been repeatedly demonstrated (L. S. Fuchs, Fuchs, & Hamlett, 1989, 1994; L. S. Fuchs, Fuchs, Hamlett, & Allinder, 1989; L. S. Fuchs, Fuchs, Hamlett, & Stecker, 1991). To illustrate, CBM may be used to assess improvement in oral reading fluency over first grade (see Mathes et al., 1998). A set of 400-word stories of middle-first-grade difficulty are used to this end. Each week, students read aloud one of these stories for 1 min to a teacher or a teacher's aide who calculates a score corresponding to the number of words read correctly. The sensitivity of CBM to student change is illustrated by the fact that, for the average student, the number of words read correctly more than triples between the beginning and end of a 16-week reading intervention (Mathes, Torgesen, & Allor, 2001).

A MULTILEVEL RESPONSE TO NONRESPONDERS

Compared to one-to-one tutoring intervention, First-Grade PALS is a low-intensity program; instruction is provided by peers and only for a limited time. It should come as no surprise, then, that it does not eliminate learning failure. Mathes et al. (2001) reported that 21% of low-achieving first graders could still be considered nonreaders at the end of peer-tutoring activities.

To obtain a precise estimate of the proportion of nonresponders to First-Grade PALS, and to boost the reading achievement of these children, McMaster, Fuchs, Fuchs, and Compton (2002) involved a large sample of first graders ($N = 418$) in regular PALS activities. Prior to PALS implementation, scores from a Rapid Letter Naming task (see Torgesen, Wagner, & Rashotte, 1997) and teachers' perceptions were used to rank-order students according to their beginning reading skills. This led to the identification of the lowest achieving children in each class as subjects of study. Average-achieving children were also identified as a reference group. The progress of the low- and average-achieving students was then closely monitored during the first 7 weeks of PALS activities using two CBM assessments: lists of sight words and lists of nonwords (Good & Kaminski, 2001). Scores reflect, respectively, the number of correctly read words and correctly expressed phonemes in 1 min. Based on this information, individual learning rate and performance level at midintervention (i.e., end of the 7th week) were computed using growth curve analysis. Curve parameters of the average-achieving students were used to estimate the normal range of response to PALS. In keeping with the dual-discrepancy criterion, low-achieving readers were identified as nonresponders if both their learning rate and performance level fell outside this normal range (i.e., 1 *SD* below their average-achieving peers). Based on these criteria, 15.8% ($n = 66$) of all students were nonresponders after 7 weeks of regular PALS activities.

At this point, nonresponders were randomly assigned to a control group (regular PALS activities) or to one of two more intensive interventions. The selection of intensive interventions for boosting reading achievement of nonresponders was based on results of previous research demonstrating the effectiveness of one-to-one tutoring provided by a trained specialist (e.g., Torgesen et al., 1999; Vellutino et al., 1996), on the limited resources typically available in schools, and on the ubiquitous policy of educating the largest possible number of children in the mainstream classroom (e.g., President's Commission on Excellence in Special Education, 2002). One of the two more intensive interventions offered to nonresponders was a modified version of PALS (modified PALS). Modified PALS activities were designed to match the skills of struggling readers with a slower pace and an emphasis on phonological awareness and decoding skills. Nonresponders in this condition were paired with a teacher-selected peer who demonstrated both good reading skills and an ability to work well with lower performing students.

The second intensive intervention was one-to-one tutoring provided by a trained research assistant (tutoring). Tutoring activities were conducted outside the classroom, in place of regular PALS activities. Tutors were trained to teach to mastery and spent more time on activities that were especially difficult for the students. As an additional motivational component, students set goals for each session and graphed their progress. Tutoring was conceptualized as a more intensive and individualized program than Modified PALS.

Due to attrition after random assignment, there were respectively 20, 15, and 21 students with complete data in each of three conditions (i.e., PALS, modified PALS, and tutoring). Research staff continued to monitor the performance of the nonresponders with the two CBM measures for 9 additional weeks. Growth curve analysis was again used to determine if students were still not responding according to the dual-discrepancy criterion. The percentage of nonresponders was 50% for the tutoring condition, 75% for modified PALS, and 81% for regular PALS. Although the difference among tutoring, modified PALS, and PALS may be important in practical terms, it failed to reach statistical significance due, in all likelihood, to the small numbers of students and low power. Overall, 9% of all students in the sample remained nonresponders at the end of the study.

RESPONSE TO NONRESPONDERS AND THE SPECIAL
EDUCATION SERVICE DELIVERY SYSTEM

Despite the general effectiveness of programs introduced into mainstream classrooms, many children continue to struggle to acquire the skills necessary to become proficient readers. Indeed, as many as 30% of children at risk for reading difficulties and as many as 50% of those with special needs fail to benefit from generally effective instruction (see Al Otaiba & Fuchs, 2002). This brings us back to our starting question: Can something be done to prevent the repeated failures that students like Josh encounter in their struggle to become competent readers? Based on the information presented in this article, if Josh received an early exposure to a state-of-the-art empirically validated best practice, he would have roughly one chance out of two to reach near-average reading proficiency by the end of second grade, a far better prospect than he currently faces.

In a sense, studying nonresponsiveness to a generally effective reading program is like seeing the proverbial glass as half empty. We risk ignoring hard-won progress and, more important, discounting important innovative instructional strategies. This being said, like others before us (e.g., Torgesen, 2000), we assert that practitioners must look closely at effectiveness data if they are to meet the goal of ensuring that all children acquire adequate reading skills in elementary school (Lyon, Alexander, & Yaffee, 1997). All children will not be served even when teachers accurately implement the best instructional practices. Although we note the limitations of our best practices, there is a positive message in the data we reviewed: Our knowledge base on identification of nonresponders is rapidly expanding, and a feasible and effective service delivery model for helping these children is emerging.

We believe that the dual-discrepancy criterion applied to CBM is an empirically sound and feasible strategy to identify nonresponders. This strategy has the advantage of explicitly taking into account learning or lack thereof—a defining feature of learning disability—and encouraging a critical examination of current instructional practices. As such, it could help practitioners devise interventions that boost the reading achievement of struggling readers and distinguish truly disabled children from children who have received inadequate instruction, highlighting the cognitive and language processing of the former (Al Otaiba & Fuchs, 2002; Clay, 1987; Vellutino et al., 1996). Dual discrepancy is also relevant to a formal diagnosis of learning disability based on a responsiveness-to-intervention definition (D. Fuchs et al., 2003). We recognize that, although promising, our work on the dual-discrepancy criterion is at an early stage. It remains to be seen if children identified as nonresponders represent a qualitatively distinct group or, alternatively, if nonresponsiveness is best conceived in terms of a continuum.

It would seem that a responsible approach to nonresponders, characterized by the dual-discrepancy criterion or otherwise, should include multiple levels of increasingly intensive and integrated interventions (see McMaster et al., 2002). Such an approach must start with the improvement of general education. The distinction between responders and nonresponders is valid only when generally effective reading programs have been implemented with fidelity for the whole class. This level of intervention can be conceived of as a primary intervention strategy (L. S. Fuchs & Fuchs, 2001). It incorporates instructional principles that address the needs of low achievers and students with learning disabilities while benefiting average- and high-achieving students. Feasibility is an equally important issue (see D. Fuchs, Fuchs, Thompson, Al Otaiba, et al., 2001). The PALS program was accordingly designed to ensure that teachers could easily, accurately, and independently implement its activities within their typical routine (D. Fuchs et al., 1997).

Because of the relatively low levels of intensity of primary interventions, a sizable portion of children will not respond. Nonresponders need access to a second level of intervention (e.g., prereferral intervention), whereby general education is modified in ways that are feasible for the teacher and unobtrusive for classmates. The goal here is to effect better student progress with minimal invasiveness to targeted nonresponders and with minimal disruption to others. Modified PALS was a first form of secondary intervention in the McMaster et al. (2002) study. It appeared to be relatively ineffective (75% of students in this condition remained nonresponders). Specific implementation features may have contributed to this outcome. Only minimal training was offered to teachers and peer tutors of nonresponding students. In addition, given that they had an entire class to oversee at the same time, it is unclear whether teachers and research staff were able to ensure that modified PALS was conducted correctly. Although this illustrates how providing nonresponders with more individualized and intensive instruction in the context of the regular classroom is a delicate balancing act, it must not be inferred that secondary prevention is inherently ineffective. The key to effective intervention of this kind may lie, for instance, in the resourceful use of teaching assistants in the context of a structured program.

If a low-cost intervention like modified PALS fails, a more intensive secondary intervention needs to be considered. Individualized attention requiring special resources may be brought to bear. It is accordingly not practical for most students and probably not desirable given that normally developing children, by definition, progress well in more naturally occurring educational environments, which also provide social benefits and are less expensive to implement. In the McMaster et al. (2002) study, one-to-one tutoring by a trained specialist outside of the classroom was the other form of secondary intervention. Despite low statistical power, results suggest that this form of tutoring is the more effective intervention to accelerate the learning rate of previously struggling readers. This of course is not surprising given the numerous studies demonstrating the general success of this approach (e.g., Torgesen et al., 1999; Vellutino et al., 1996).

We want to stress that even if one-to-one tutoring succeeded for every child, which is not the case (McMaster et al., 2002; Torgesen, 2000), the problem of nonresponsiveness could not be considered solved because schools would still have to identify children eligible for this kind of intervention, which can necessarily be offered to only a small minority. Indeed, maximally effective general education practices (primary intervention) and low-cost secondary intervention are required, if only to strategically allocate struggling readers to one-to-one tutoring or other forms of labor-intensive and costly interventions conducted outside the classroom. It is quite conceivable that a sizable portion of struggling readers that happened to respond well to this last type of intervention would have benefited from more cost-efficient intervention efforts. What is needed is an integrated array of increasingly individualized, intensive, and effective interventions, both to provide students with appropriate instruction given their individual needs and to control the costs associated with special education. We do not mean to imply that funding for special education could or should be cut back. It must be realized that with efficient primary and low-cost secondary intervention efforts, the number of children referred to end-of-the-line services would decline, but the proportion of more seriously disabled children served would rise. Inadequate funding of tertiary intervention services such as special education would mean giving up hope for these children.

REFERENCES

Adams, M. J. (1990). *Beginning to read: Thinking and learning about print.* Cambridge, MA: MIT Press.

Al Otaiba, S., & Fuchs, D. (2002). Characteristics of children who are unresponsive to early literacy intervention. *Remedial and Special Education, 23,* 300–316.

Clay, M. N. (1987). Learning to be learning disabled. *New Zealand Journal of Educational Studies, 22,* 155–173.

Cunningham, A. E., & Stanovich, K. E. (1998). What reading does for the mind. *American Educator, 22,* 8–15.

Deno, S. L. (1985). Curriculum-based measurement: The emerging alternative. *Exceptional Children, 52,* 219–232.

Foorman, B. R., Francis, D. J., Fletcher, J. M., Schatschneider, C., & Mehta, P. (1998). The role of instruction in learning to read: Preventing reading failure in at-risk children. *Journal of Educational Psychology, 90,* 37–55.

Francis, D. J., Shaywitz, S. E., Stuebing, K. K., Shaywitz, B. A., & Fletcher, J. M. (1996). Developmental lag versus deficit models of reading disability: A longitudinal, individual growth curves analysis. *Journal of Educational Psychology, 88,* 3–17.

Fuchs, D., Fuchs, L. S., Mathes, P., & Simmons, D. C. (1997). Peer-assisted learning strategies: Making classrooms more responsive to diversity. *American Educational Research Journal, 34,* 174–206.

Fuchs, D., Fuchs, L. S., Thompson, A., Al Otaiba, S., Yen, L., Yang, N. J., et al. (2001). Is reading important in reading-readiness programs? A randomized field trial with teachers as program implementers. *Journal of Educational Psychology, 93,* 251–267.

Fuchs, D., Fuchs, L. S., Thompson, A., Svenson, E., Yen, L., Al Otaiba, S., et al. (2001). Peer-assisted learning strategies in reading: Extensions for kindergarten, first grade, and high school. *Remedial and Special Education, 22,* 15–21.

Fuchs, D., Fuchs, L. S., Yen, L., McMaster, K., Svenson, E., Yang, N., et al. (2001). Developing first-grade reading fluency through peer mediation. *Teaching Exceptional Children, 32,* 90–93.

Fuchs, D., Mock, D., Morgan, P. L., & Young, C. L. (2003). Responsiveness-to-intervention: Definitions, evidence, and implications for the learning disabilities construct. *Learning Disabilities Research & Practice, 18,* 157–171.

Fuchs, L. S., & Fuchs, D. (1998). Treatment validity: A unifying concept for reconceptualizing the identification of learning disabilities. *Learning Disabilities Research & Practice, 13,* 204–219.

Fuchs, L. S., & Fuchs, D. (2001). Principles for the prevention and intervention of mathematics difficulties. *Learning Disabilities Research & Practice, 16,* 85–95.

Fuchs, L. S., Fuchs, D., & Hamlett, C. L. (1989). Effects of alternative goal structures within curriculum-based measurement. *Exceptional Children, 55,* 429–438.

Fuchs, L. S., Fuchs, D., & Hamlett, C. L. (1994). Strengthening the connection between assessment and instructional planning with expert system. *Exceptional Children, 61,* 138–146.

Fuchs, L. S., Fuchs, D., Hamlett, C. L., & Allinder, R. M. (1989). The reliability and validity of skills analysis within curriculum-based measurement. *Diagnostique, 14,* 203–221.

Fuchs, L. S., Fuchs, D., Hamlett, C. L., & Stecker, P. M. (1991). Effects of curriculum-based measurement and consultation on teacher planning and student achievement in mathematics operations. *American Educational Research Journal, 28,* 617–641.

Fuchs, L. S., Fuchs, D., & Speece, D. L. (2002). Treatment validity as a unifying construct for identifying learning disabilities. *Learning Disability Quarterly, 25,* 33–45.

Good, R. H., & Kaminski, R. A. (Eds.). (2001). *Dynamic indicators of basic early literacy skills* (5th ed.). Eugene, OR: Institute for the Development of Educational Achievement.

Good, R. H., Kaminsky, R., & Shinn, M. (1999, January). *Growth and development indicators: From development to refinement and back again.* Paper presented at the Pacific Coast Research Conference, San Diego, CA.

Greenwood, C. R., Delquadri, J. C., & Hall, R. V. (1989). Longitudinal effects of classwide peer tutoring. *Journal of Educational Psychology, 81,* 371–383.

Hatcher, P. J., Hulme, C., & Ellis, A. W. (1994). Ameliorating early reading failure by integrating the teaching of reading and phonological skills: The phonological linkage hypothesis. *Child Development, 65,* 41–57.

Juel, C. (1988). Learning to read and write: A longitudinal study of 54 children from first through fourth grades. *Journal of Educational Psychology, 80,* 437–447.

Lyon, G. R., Alexander, D., & Yaffee, S. (1997). Progress and promise in research in learning disabilities. *Learning Disabilities: A Multidisciplinary Journal, 8,* 1–6.

Mathes, P. G., & Fuchs, L. S. (1994). The efficacy of peer tutoring in reading for students with mild disabilities: A best-evidence synthesis. *School Psychology Review, 23,* 59–80.

Mathes, P. G., Howard, J. K., Allen, S., & Fuchs, D. (1998). Peer-assisted learning strategies for first-grade readers: Making early reading instruction more responsive to the needs of diverse learners. *Reading Research Quarterly, 33,* 62–95.

Mathes, P. G., Torgesen, J. K., & Allor, J. H. (2001). The effects of peer-assisted literacy strategies for first-grade readers with and without additional computer-assisted instruction in phonological awareness. *American Educational Research Journal, 38,* 371–410.

McMaster, K., Fuchs, D., Fuchs, L. S., & Compton, D. (2002). Monitoring the academic progress of children who are unresponsive to generally effective early reading intervention. *Assessment for Effective Intervention, 27,* 23–33.

National Institute of Child Health and Human Development. (2000). *Report of the National Reading Panel: Teaching children to read: An evidence-based assessment of the scientific research literature on reading and its implications for reading instruction* (NIH Publication No. 00–4769). Washington, DC: Author.

O'Connor, R. E., Notari-Syverson, A., & Vadasy, P. F. (1996). Ladders to literacy: The effects of teacher-led phonological activities in kindergarten for children with and without mild disabilities. *Exceptional Children, 63,* 117–130.

O'Connor, R. E., Notari-Syverson, A., & Vadasy, P. F. (1998). First-grade effects of teacher-led phonological activities in kindergarten for children with mild disabilities: A follow-up study. *Learning Disabilities Research & Practice, 13,* 43–52.

President's Commission on Excellence in Special Education. (2002). *A new era: Revitalizing special education for children and their families.* Retrieved December 1, 2002, from http://www.ed.gov/inits/commissions boards/whspecialeducation/index.html

Pressley, M. (2002). *Reading instruction that works: The case for balanced teaching* (2nd ed.). New York: Guilford.

Rashotte, C. A., MacPhee, K., & Torgesen, J. K. (2001). The effectiveness of a group reading instruction program with poor readers in multiple grades. *Learning Disability Quarterly, 24,* 119–134.

Rosenshine, B., & Meister, C. (1994). Reciprocal teaching: A review of the research. *Review of Educational Research, 64,* 479–530.

Simmons, D. C., Fuchs, D., Fuchs, L. S., Hodge, J. P., & Mathes, P. G. (1994). Importance of instructional complexity and role reciprocity to classwide peer tutoring. *Learning Disabilities Research & Practice, 9,* 203–212.

Smith, M. C. (1998). *Literacy for the twenty-first century: Research, policy, practices, and the National Adult Literacy Survey.* Westport, CT: Praeger.

Snow, C. E., Burns, M. S., & Griffin, P. (1998). *Preventing reading difficulties in young children.* Washington, DC: National Academy Press.

Speece, D. L., & Case, L. P. (2001). Classification in context: An alternative approach to identifying early reading disability. *Journal of Educational Psychology, 93,* 735–749.

Torgesen, J. K. (2000). Individual differences in response to early interventions in reading: The lingering problem of treatment resisters. *Learning Disabilities Research & Practice, 15,* 55–64.

Torgesen, J. K., & Davis, C. (1996). Individual difference variables that predict response to training in phonological awareness. *Journal of Experimental Child Psychology, 63,* 1–21.

Torgesen, J. K., Wagner, R. K., & Rashotte, C. A. (1997). Prevention and remediation of severe reading disabilities: Keeping the end in mind. *Scientific Studies of Reading, 1,* 217–234.

Torgesen, J. K., Wagner, R. K., Rashotte, C. A., Lindamood, P., Rose, E., Conway, T., et al. (1999). Preventing reading failure in young children with phonological processing disabilities: Group and individual responses to instruction. *Journal of Educational Psychology, 91,* 579–593.

Uhry, J. K., & Shepherd, M. J. (1997). Teaching phonological recoding to young children with phonological processing deficits: The effect on sight-vocabulary acquisition. *Learning Disability Quarterly, 20,* 104–125.

Vellutino, F. R., Scanlon, D. M., Sipay, E. R., Small, S., Chen, R., Pratt, A., et al. (1996). Cognitive profiles of difficult-to-remediate and readily remediated poor readers: Early intervention as a vehicle for distinguishing between cognitive and experiential deficits as basic causes of specific reading disability. *Journal of Educational Psychology, 88,* 601–638.

Toward a Science
of Professional Development
in Early Reading Instruction

David J. Chard
Special Education Area
University of Oregon

In the current climate of accountability and research-based practices in reading instruction, professional development is often identified as one of the key elements needed to change the trajectory of progress for struggling readers and to ensure their ongoing success. Research on teacher quality and its impact on student achievement seems to suggest that teacher quality has a significant effect on student academic achievement. Although enhancing teachers' effectiveness has been the subject of much interest and fascinating speculation, there has been little empirical research to document the factors that make professional development optimally effective. The purpose of this article is to propose a conceptual framework of factors that support professional development and sustain its impact on reading improvement. In addition, I suggest several important questions that could be answered if a science of professional development is realized.

Successfully teaching children to read is one of the most important functions of schools. Despite increased interest, expanded fiscal allocations by local, state, and federal education agencies, and heightened political attention, reading outcomes for many children remain disappointingly inadequate (National Center for Educational Statistics, 2000). One explanation for low reading outcomes stems from the inability of schools and teachers to meet the needs of struggling readers, many of whom will eventually be identified as requiring special education. Despite important intended outcomes of specialized remedial reading programs for struggling readers, very often students who are demonstrating difficulties in reading in the primary grades do not improve (Juel, 1988; Torgesen et al., 1999).

In the current climate of accountability and research-based practices in reading instruction, professional development is often identified as one of the key elements needed to change the trajectory of progress for struggling readers and to ensure their ongoing success. Moreover, research on teacher quality and its impact on student achievement

Requests for reprints should be sent to David J. Chard, Special Education Area, 5261 University of Oregon, Eugene, OR 97403. E-mail: dchard@uoregon.edu seems to suggest that teacher quality has a significant effect on student academic achievement (Whitehurst, 2002).

Enhancing teachers' effectiveness has been the subject of much interest and fascinating speculation. In part, this is because many teachers enter the classroom unprepared for the complex work of teaching. As Elmore (2002) noted: "Most people who currently work in public schools weren't hired to do this work, nor have they been adequately prepared to do it either by their professional education or by their prior experience in schools" (p. 3). Unfortunately, surprisingly little empirical research has been conducted on effective methods of providing in-service or preservice professional development in specific research-based knowledge and skills related to reading instruction (Gersten, Chard, & Baker, 2000). Particularly missing from research are studies that systematically examine the effects of teacher training on student outcomes.

For this article, I define professional development as the efforts in which schools engage to improve in-service teachers' reading instruction for the full range of learners. Although we understand that improving professional development is a task shared with agencies, both traditional and alternative, that certify preservice teachers, the efficacy of preservice certification programs, although enormously important (Darling-Hammond & Young, 2002), is beyond the scope of this article. In addition, although any proposals to improve professional development should not be undertaken naively and in the absence of improvement in teacher certification programs, we have tried to address those issues in other papers (Chard, 1999).

The science of teaching reading has outpaced the science of professional development in reading instruction. In fact, there is a long history of research on pedagogical practices in reading (e.g., Brophy, 1983; Chard & Kame'enui, 2000; Grossman, Valencia, & Hamel, 1995; Pressley et al., 2001). Ironically, we know much more about what needs to be changed than how to put the changes in place. The National Reading Panel (2000) conducted an extensive meta-analysis of reading research. More than 300 studies on the topic of professional development were identified. However, only 21 studies met the methodological criteria for inclusion in their review. Because of the wide range of variables studied in those 21 studies, meta-analytic approaches to data analysis could not be used. Thus, a meta-analysis of professional development practices in early reading outcomes providing findings and their impact is not available.

Despite the lack of a scientific knowledge base on professional development approaches in reading instruction, schools engage in a wide range of professional development activities annually. We estimate that schools spend billions of dollars on professional development activities each year. The unstated intent of these activities is to improve school and teacher effectiveness in hopes of improving student achievement. However, change is generally regarded as positive even when it achieves no discernible results (Elmore, 2002).

The focus of this article is on a proposal for studying professional development in reading instruction that results in meaningful improvement for struggling readers. The specific purpose of this article is to propose a conceptual framework of factors that support professional development and sustain its impact on reading improvement. In addition, several important questions are posed that could be answered if a science of professional development is realized.

THE CONTEXT FOR IMPROVING
PROFESSIONAL DEVELOPMENT

I would be remiss to begin a discussion about enhancing instruction for struggling read- ers without a clear connection to the context in which professional development occurs. In fact, it has been argued that all too often we have attempted to solve school achieve- ment issues by focusing on the professional knowledge and skills of teachers without considering the contextual variables that support and sustain improvements in teaching and learning (Elmore, 2002). Although important efforts to improve teachers' knowl- edge and skills in teaching reading may be imperative to improving reading outcomes, these efforts could be thwarted if not accompanied by attention to other important con- textual variables. As Elmore noted about the gap between research and practice: "It is not so much about knowing what good professional development looks like; it's knowing how to get it rooted in the institutional structure of schools" (p. 12).

Torgesen (2003) asserted that there are at least six reasons why schools are not yet able to successfully teach struggling readers to read. These reasons include:

1. Many elementary schools are not organized or focused in ways that most effec- tively promote literacy for all children.
2. Many schools do not really expect students from low wealth or minority back- grounds to learn to read well.
3. Teachers often do not possess the special knowledge or teaching skills to effec- tively teach students who are experiencing difficulties learning to read.
4. Teachers often do not have adequate materials or instructional time available to them to effectively promote literacy for all their students.
5. Many families and neighborhood environments do not provide experiences that prepare children to learn to read well.
6. There is significant variability in the oral language capacity of students entering schools.

These explanations for low performance in reading are interdependent and require a larger focus on schoolwide reading that includes contextual factors related to school improvement.

The system of professional development employed by most schools today ignores contextual variables that might aid in the institutionalization of improvement. The nature and content of professional development in reading was described by the Commission on Reading (1984) in *Becoming a Nation of Readers*. The Commission described a system of professional development in which "almost all teachers take additional university courses ... subscribe to professional magazines ... and attend at least one professional conference or workshop a year" (p. 110). Despite what seemed like adequate measures to ensure increasing expertise in teachers' knowledge and skills, the Commission noted that this system was flawed. The system of professional development prevalent in public schools today has not changed substantially since the Commission's report. Further- more, we wonder whether the suggestions provided by the Commission would be suffi- cient even if they were implemented.

TABLE 1
Conceptual Framework of Systemic and Personal Variables
Related to Professional Development (Gilbert, 1978)

Variable	Information	Instrumentation	Motivation
System	Data 1. Relevant and frequent performance feedback 2. Aligned with standards	Tools, materials, and technology designed scientifically to meet the educational needs of struggling readers	Incentives 1. Contingent on performance 2. Include career-development opportunities
Person	Knowledge 1. Scientifically designed to match exemplary performance 2. Differentiated based on teachers' needs	Capacity 1. Focused on procedural skills 2. Include coaching support 3. Differentiated based on teachers' needs	Motives 1. Responsive to teachers' sense of efficacy

To frame the complex context in which professional development is situated, I draw on a model for developing human competence offered by Gilbert (1978) more than 25 years ago (see Table 1). The conceptual framework comprised several important contextual factors, which Gilbert separated into system variables and person variables related to improvement in competence or performance. Within each of these categories of variables, Gilbert proposed three variable types: information, instrumentation, and motivation. He also proposed that the system variables were of higher priority than person variables because they set the occasion for individual competence to be developed. Although Gilbert's model lacks empirical support, it does provide anchors that help us to consider improvement efforts. In the following section, each of Gilbert's proposed variables is described in the context of professional development for reading instruction.

SYSTEM VARIABLES

Information: Data on Valued and Measurable Outcomes

The first system variable related to improvement in competence is having shared values and agreement on measurable outcomes and a process for collecting data to assess student reading performance. Improved reading outcomes for students may be difficult to achieve because of what Torgesen (2003) referred to as a lack of a shared vision or focus with clearly specified and valued outcomes. In Gilbert's (1978) model, these outcomes are measured frequently and used to make changes toward improvement. Until the mid-1990s, little agreement existed about what outcomes should be measured in reading instruction. However, several synthesis documents of the empirical research on how children learn to read have yielded greater consensus about reading instruction and assessment (Adams, 1990; Committee on the Prevention of Reading Difficulties, 1998; National Reading Panel, 2000). Consequently, determining the measurable and valued outcomes for teaching and monitoring reading is much more tenable. In fact, the certainty about our knowledge base in reading instruction has led to national and federal initiatives to ensure that "no child is left behind."

The valued and measurable outcomes described in Gilbert's (1978) model are those that are proximal to teacher and student behavior and responsive to daily instruction. For example, if a teacher were spending his or her instructional time teaching students how to employ a decoding strategy to read unfamiliar words, he or she would want the measures to indicate progress in learning to read targeted words.

Effective professional development would link training and implementation of progress monitoring tools that related to the instructional elements of reading that are essential at that grade level. For example, using the Dynamic Indicators of Basic Early Literacy Skills (DIBELS; Kaminski & Good, 1998), teachers can accurately assess their students' progress on measures that are designed to be sensitive to the specific skills that are being taught. In kindergarten, for example, where the focus of instruction is, in part, on the development of phonemic awareness, DIBELS can be used to assess students' phonemic segmentation fluency. DIBELS allows teachers to gauge progress toward specific benchmarks in phonemic segmentation fluency and can also provide valuable information about which phonemes students are consistently missing and whether rate of segmentation is adequate. From a school- or districtwide perspective, the DIBELS assessments can pinpoint classrooms and schools where students are not making adequate progress. This feature will be important as we address the need for professional development that is differentiated based on specific teachers' needs.

Instrumentation: Tools and Resources

The second system factor outlined in Gilbert's (1978) model involves the tools available for reading instruction. For reading, these tools and resources comprise instructional materials, time, personnel support, and technology. Prior to the late 1990s, instructional materials and technology were largely created based on market demand. If the conventional approaches to teaching reading were focused on a particular approach, publishers and software developers were compelled to respond to market demands to sell their products. This began to change when Texas and California created frameworks for reading instruction that required that instructional materials and technology meet finely wrought standards for teaching reading and language arts. Moreover, these requirements resulted in some publishers deciding not to submit materials for review in those states.

Although the actions of state departments like Texas and California were dramatic, criticism of published materials to teach reading have been widely published in the research literature for many years. These criticisms have focused mainly on the lack of alignment between research-based instructional principles and the instructional approaches advocated in the published materials (e.g., Jitendra, Chard, Hoppes, Renouf, & Cardill, 2001; Smith et al., 2001). As a result of the circumstances in Texas and California and subsequent requirements of the federal Reading First Initiative, publishers are under increasing pressure to provide materials that are more closely aligned with research findings and meet the needs of a wider range of readers.

The importance of effectively designed instructional materials and technology should not be underestimated. Several studies have documented the differential effects favoring materials that are aligned with research-based principles when contrasted with alternative instructional approaches across a range of literacy activities (e.g., Beck, McKeown, Sandora, Kucan, & Worthy, 1996; Foorman, Fletcher, Francis, Schatschneider, & Mehta, 1998; O'Connor, Jenkins, & Slocum, 1995). The benefits of core reading materials (i.e., a commercial reading program) that include explicit instructional strategies, coordinated instructional sequences, and ample practice in aligned student materials may be many, including improved student performance (Rayner, Foorman, Perfetti, Pesetsky, & Seidenberg, 2001) as well as unintended professional development. For example, Brabham and Villaume (2002) noted that "many seasoned teachers commented that their abilities to teach phonics flexibly and responsively were grounded in experiences they had as novices working with reading programs that featured a systematic phonics component" (p. 439). Thus, the materials serve as a professional development tool in addition to serving instruction directly.

In addition to the published materials used to teach reading, schools must consider the time needed to adequately teach reading and language arts effectively. Historically, the time frame for teaching reading was approximately 1 to 1.5 hr per day. However, this time frame may be insufficient depending on students' ages and instructional needs. There is little evidence of the exact amount of instructional time needed to optimize reading growth. However, it has been suggested that schools need to protect instructional time to prevent it from eroding away to irrelevant school activities (e.g., assemblies, announcements). In addition, there is emerging evidence that students who are struggling to learn to read need significantly more instructional time than those who are developing typically (Torgesen et al., 1999).

The relation between professional development and the tools used to teach reading is underestimated. Because teachers' instructional practices are, in part, dependent on their instructional tools, efforts to enhance teachers' effectiveness in the absence of effective tools (e.g., effectively designed materials, adequate time) may make the task not just more difficult but impossible.

Motivation: Incentives for Professional Improvement

The success or failure of professional development efforts is based on many critical elements, not the least of which is whether there are appropriate incentives to support use of the knowledge and skills provided. One incentive for ensuring participation and perhaps motivation to use knowledge provided during professional development opportunities is to provide incentives to teachers for the extra time and effort that is required to attend and implement targeted instructional practices.

Klingner, Vaughn, Hughes, and Arguelles (1999) examined the sustained use of reading practices by teachers who had participated in a yearlong professional development program. Several years later, these teachers were observed teaching these practices and individually interviewed. Six of the seven teachers sustained one or more of the three practices at a high rate. Teachers identified factors that served as "incentives" or support for sustaining reading practices and factors that interfered with their sustained use of the reading practices. The following factors were perceived as supports or incentives:

- *Development of a support network that included other teachers using the instructional practice:* Teachers perceived that they were more likely to sustain an instructional practice in reading when they had other teachers or researchers available to discuss what they were doing and resolve issues. Teachers particularly valued having other teachers to share ideas and resolve problems.
- *Principal support for the instructional practice:* Teachers overwhelmingly identified administrative support as a necessary factor for implementing and maintaining instructional practices in reading. Teachers indicated that when their principals consistently supported what was taught in professional development, they implemented and maintained the practices.
- *Documentation that students were benefiting from the practice:* Teachers indicated that they were much more inclined to use a practice if there was very clear and believable evidence to them that their students were benefiting academically from the use of the practice. Teachers indicated that they continued to use an instructional practice because they were able to document clear gains in reading and writing.
- *Student acceptance of the instructional practice:* Teachers revealed that students' perceptions of the practice influenced whether they used it and how often. Although students did not need to overwhelmingly like it, they had to find it at least palatable.
- *Flexibility in modifying and adapting the practice:* Teachers indicated that they valued instructional practices that lent themselves to modification for their classes and students. They did not want to implement practices rigidly with no adjustments.
- *Materials readily available to use:* Teachers reported that they were unable to spend time searching for appropriate materials or redesigning materials. They needed all of the materials, copies, and books readily accessible.
- *Instructional practices enhanced outcomes on high-stakes assessments:* Teachers indicated that high-stakes assessments influenced their instruction and that professional development that highlighted practices that would enhance their teaching in relation to students' outcomes was valued and likely to be used.

The close alignment of instructional tools to the measured outcomes may result in improved reading achievement for the vast majority of learners. The rewards of this improved achievement may be the single best internal incentive schools can provide to their faculties. Gilbert (1978) argued that improving the competence of individuals within an organization, such as the school, would be enhanced if these system variables were first addressed from the beginning.

PERSON VARIABLES

Having established the need for systemic support for professional development, I turn to the person variables in Gilbert's (1978) competence model. Specifically, I suggest three areas, at least intuitively, to be at the heart of any effort to provide professional development aimed at improving reading instruction for struggling readers: teacher knowledge, teacher capacity, and teachers' sense of efficacy.

Information: Subject Matter and Pedagogical Knowledge

The relative importance of teachers' subject matter knowledge versus general pedagogical knowledge has been recently discussed in policy reports (Whitehurst, 2002) and research syntheses (Darling-Hammond & Young, 2002). In my experience, any argument in favor of one type of knowledge being paramount is misguided. Rather, I suggest that teacher knowledge includes (a) specific domain knowledge about teaching reading, and (b) general understanding of how to teach different types of knowledge (e.g., skills, concepts, strategies) effectively. Specific knowledge and skills about teaching reading relate to foundational knowledge of how children learn to read and what key instructional areas facilitate their reading progress. In contrast, general pedagogical knowledge assists teachers to plan instruction commensurate with the nature of the knowledge forms being taught and to make decisions about the sequence and timing of instruction. Each of these knowledge areas is discussed briefly in the next sections.

Subject matter knowledge.   Papers, books, technical reports, and professional development guides have articulated specific documented effective practices in which teachers should engage to improve student reading achievement. To address adequately the range of knowledge and skills covered in these publications and tools is well beyond the scope of this article. Although there is an emerging knowledge base on the level of domain knowledge that teachers possess, little is known about the relation between teachers' domain knowledge and their actual instructional effectiveness in the classroom (Bos, Mather, Dickson, Podhajski, & Chard, 2001; McCutchen et al., 2002; Moats, 1994).

Rather than attempt to summarize all of the knowledge and skill areas that are critical to understanding the development of reading and providing examples of specific sources of information about each of these areas, I highly recommend that preservice and in-service teachers study and apply knowledge from several recently published documents on reading, including *Beginning to Read: Thinking and Learning About Print* (Adams, 1990), *Preventing Reading Difficulties in Young Children* (Committee on the Prevention of Reading Difficulties, 1998), *Minority Students in Special and Gifted Education* (National Research Council, 2002), *Teaching Children to Read* (National Reading Panel, 2000), and *Put Reading First* (Armbruster, Lehr, & Osborn, 2001). These five documents combined could serve as a school's resources for what needs to be taught to improve overall reading achievement. In addition, they could be used as a stimulus for a long-term professional development effort to improve the overall effectiveness of reading instruction.

In addition to these publications, I recommend that schools consider reviewing resources developed specifically to provide professional development to teachers on reading development. For example, the Texas Center for Reading and Language Arts has produced several professional development guides on effective reading instruction from pre-K through the intermediate grades (see http://www.texasreading.org/tcrla/index .htm). Similarly, the National Center to Improve the Tools of Educators has developed professional development materials that focus on reading instruction and assessment at the primary grades (see http://idea.uoregon.edu/~ibr/). Both of these resources could be used to enhance teachers' subject matter knowledge.

General pedagogical knowledge.   Effective teachers understand both the nature of the content they are teaching and the effect a teacher's behavior can have on students' learning.

Teachers frequently overemphasize particular practices rather than allow the knowledge that is being taught to influence, if not dictate, the design of the instruction. For example, it is still common practice in many classrooms across the country for teachers to encourage children to use multiple strategies (e.g., context clues, prediction based on the first sound in a word) for initially reading unfamiliar words rather than explicitly teaching students to blend the sounds or word parts to identify the word (Adams, 1999; Ehri, 1995). Similarly, it has been common practice for decades to teach comprehension by asking students a series of questions after reading a selection of text. Both of these practices ignore an important insight regarding instructional design. Specifically, the design of instruction should be dictated by the nature of the content being taught.

An example of how the content can dictate the instructional design is in the area of strategy instruction. Strategy instruction involves giving children an action plan for how to negotiate complex areas of academic learning such as reading comprehension. The action plans have been described as procedural facilitators, prompts, or scaffolds (Rosenshine, 1997). What sets strategy instruction apart from teaching a discrete skill such as the sound associated with the letter *m,* for example, is that although we may learn the steps of a strategy in one lesson, we continue to refine our use of strategies throughout our lifetime. In other words, after students are introduced to cognitive strategies, they use them often and receive specific feedback on their use so that they may become increasingly automatic in both identifying when and where to use them and how to use them effectively.

An example of effective cognitive strategy instruction is in the area of text structure. Text structures refer to the common features of specific types of text. For example, narrative text structure or story grammar includes the common features of a story such as the main character, setting, problem, solution, and theme. Another example is persuasive text structure. Features of this type of text often include a proposition, supporting arguments, opposing arguments, and refutations of the opposing arguments. Some students learn text features by listening to and discussing texts with adults and peers. Many students, including those with cognitive disabilities, benefit from having these text features made explicit. Explicitly teaching text structure has been shown to enhance the reading comprehension of many students including those with disabilities (Gersten, Fuchs, Williams, & Baker, 2001; Gurney, Gersten, Dimino, & Carnine, 1990; Idol & Croll, 1987).

Educational research in the 1970s and 1980s was dominated by observations of effective classrooms. The result of those studies was professional development that urged teachers to use practices that were used by effective teachers. However, these professional development efforts often failed to sustain improvements in teaching because they did not focus on teachers' understanding of why the practices were effective and how they would benefit their students (Gersten et al., 2001; Kennedy, 1991; Richardson, 1994). Despite the lack of sustained implementation, many of these behaviors were indeed effective at improving student outcomes.

The following effective instructional behaviors (Rosenshine, 1997) are associated with improved outcomes for struggling learners, including students with disabilities:

- Provide students with a range of examples.
- Provide students with explicit models of proficient performance.
- Provide students with multiple opportunities to explain how and why they proceeded in a particular way.
- Provide frequent and ongoing feedback on student progress.
- Provide adequate support so that students persist in learning.
- Provide adequate practice with activities that are engaging.
- Measure and control the difficulty of the task, providing challenges as well as frequent opportunities for success.

Explicitness helps promote these effective instructional behaviors. Making instruction visible and explicit is an essential feature of effective interventions for students with disabilities and other struggling learners (Elbaum, Vaughn, Hughes, & Moody, 1999; Gersten & Baker, 2001). Whether it is the explicit teaching of the steps in the writing process (for a review, see Swanson & Hoskyn, 1998; Wong, 2000) or the use of "think alouds" by the teacher as a means for teaching reading comprehension strategies (Klingner, Vaughn, & Schumm, 1998), students with disabilities benefit when the elements of what they are learning are identified and demonstrated with examples.

There is little doubt that teacher knowledge is a key element to improving reading outcomes for all children. In fact, without a knowledgeable teacher, the context variables described earlier would do little to help students learn to read. However, it is also important that teachers understand how and when to apply their knowledge to the assessment and instruction of individual readers.

Instrumentation: Capacity to Apply Knowledge and Use Tools in the Classroom

The second important personal variable is capacity. In Gilbert's (1978) model, capacity refers to teachers' ability to use their knowledge of reading instruction to address the daily instructional needs of struggling readers through specific teaching practices. Arguably, the knowledge most closely associated with the professional responsibilities of a reading specialist or special educator is the specific instructional knowledge developed through the supervised experience of teaching reading to struggling readers. This knowledge assists the reading teacher in anticipating, identifying, and preventing reading difficulties before they become deeper academic problems. I contend that it is this performance capacity that is necessary to move from being a teacher who can provide instruction to typically developing readers to one who can competently address the instructional needs of struggling readers.

It is a common practice to provide preservice teachers an opportunity to begin developing their capacity through supervised practice teaching. However, practicing teachers do not have these same opportunities. Many teachers have developed their capacity to recognize and address particular reading problems through trial and error over many years. However, we do not have the luxury to wait for less effective teachers to develop their capacity in this way. Rather, professional development must address the need for building capacity directly. My recommendation is that this capacity building be done in two ways: (a) learning how to effectively teach struggling readers, and (b) using effectively designed reading instructional materials.

I recommend that all teachers have highly structured learning experiences on how to teach struggling readers successfully in an intervention context under the careful supervision of a well-trained reading coach. I believe that with consistent feedback, many teachers will develop practice knowledge about working with struggling readers that they may otherwise lack. Ideally, this opportunity would include assessing students' understanding of specific skill and strategy areas, setting specific reading goals (e.g., identifying a specific number of letter–sound correspondences accurately in 1 min), planning and delivering appropriate instructional lessons to achieve the goal, monitoring student performance regularly, and adjusting instruction based on performance. This closely connected cycle of instruction, intuitive to teachers who spend their career working effectively with struggling readers, is unfamiliar to most teachers. Moreover, the intensity and demand of this instructional cycle has been documented to improve reading outcomes when implemented with students experiencing extreme difficulty in learning to read (Dickson & Bursuck, 2003; Torgesen et al., 2001).

Motivation: Teachers' Sense of General and Personal Teaching Efficacy

The third personal variable is motivation as it relates to teachers' perceptions of their effectiveness in teaching struggling readers. During the 1980s, tremendous interest developed around the influence of teachers' perceptions of their effectiveness and its influence on their teaching (Gibson & Dembo, 1984; Smylie, 1988). This interest was fueled in part by the inescapable notion that intervention effectiveness is dependent on teacher effectiveness, which, in turn, is dependent on teachers' beliefs and assumptions (Simmons, Kame'enui, & Chard, 1998). This focus on perceptions of practice relies on Bandura's (1977) early work on perceptions and their influence on human behavior. Bandura argued that human behavior, in general, is influenced by two perceptions: a general outcome perception, an estimate that a given behavior will result in a particular outcome; and a more personal efficacy expectation, a belief that one can successfully perform the behavior required to produce the outcome.

In teaching, an example of a general outcome expectation is a teacher's belief that effective reading instruction could offset the effects of a lack of early literacy experiences or of delayed oral language. This is considered a general expectation as it reflects teachers' expectations for all teachers and, therefore, may or may not reflect beliefs about their own effectiveness (Denham & Michael, 1981). A more personal efficacy expectation would be a teacher's assessment of his or her own ability to teach effectively (Simmons et al., 1998). Researchers have referred to these two belief areas as general teaching efficacy and personal teaching efficacy (Ashton & Webb, 1986; Gibson & Dembo, 1984).

What do these perceptions have to do with professional development? Students' academic achievement influences teachers' sense of general teaching efficacy, which, in turn, is related to teacher behaviors (Ashton & Webb, 1986; Hoy & Woolfolk, 1990). More specifically, if students are meeting achievement expectations, teachers perceive that these outcomes are a result of effective teaching and continue to perform effective teaching behaviors. There is also some evidence suggesting a positive linear relation between the amount of professional development and personal teaching efficacy (Hoy & Woolfolk, 1990).

Smylie (1988) extended the work on personal teaching efficacy by coupling it with a variable he referred to as certainty of practice. Smylie found that teachers who reported higher levels of certainty about the effectiveness of their practice were also the teachers with the highest levels of personal teaching efficacy. Most interesting, Smylie found that teachers with relatively high levels of personal teaching efficacy were more likely to seek innovations in their practice. The irony in Smylie's findings was that those teachers who perceived themselves as being most effective and certain about the effectiveness of their practice were the same teachers interested in finding new and more effective methods of teaching. The implication of this line of research could be that the teachers most likely to benefit from professional development efforts are those that are already effective. However, a primary limitation of Smylie's work is that it was a study of teachers' self-report rather than actual behavior and may not reflect accurate teacher perceptions.

A related line of research sheds light on the perception–behavior relation. Guskey (1989) posited a relevant theory suggesting that teacher practice changes attitudes rather than vice versa. Guskey argued that for teachers to change the way they think about a practice, they need to try the new practice with the students for whom it was designed. If the practices they try are effective, meaning they and their students are successful as a result of the practice, teachers respond favorably and are more likely to use the practice again. Moreover, Guskey reported that when teachers respond positively toward a practice, they also take more responsibility for student learning.

The broad implications of the research on perceptions and their relation to effective instruction are important. It would seem that professional development efforts to improve practice in reading instruction for struggling readers should be designed in a way that allows teachers to implement the practice with students in their classrooms. Ideally, these implementation opportunities should include coaching with feedback to ensure that the practices are implemented effectively. In addition, to influence teachers' perceptions positively, it might be very useful to view videotaped footage of their attempts to implement the new practice and the positive outcomes it elicits in students. It is important to note here how these implications parallel our recommendations regarding enhancing teachers' capacity as well as their linkage to teacher incentives.

TOWARD A SCIENCE OF PROFESSIONAL DEVELOPMENT

The state of the art in the professional development literature is represented by the National Staff Development Council's standards for professional development (Elmore, 2002). These revised standards, outlined in Table 2, are commendable in many ways. In particular, I am encouraged by the focus on student outcome data to establish professional development priorities as well as the explicit linkage between assessment and instruction. Overall, these standards provide schools with guidance in making professional development decisions. However, as has been noted on earlier occasions (Gersten et al., 2000; Vaughn,

TABLE 2
National Staff Development Council's Revised Standards for Staff Development

Context standards
  Staff development that improves the learning of all students:
  • Organizes adults into learning communities whose goals are aligned with those of the school and district
  • Requires skillful school and district leaders who guide continuous instructional improvement
  • Requires resources to support adult learning and collaboration
Process standards
  Staff development that improves the learning of all students:
  • Uses disaggregated student data to determine adult learning priorities, monitor progress, and help sustain continuous improvement
  • Uses multiple sources of information to guide improvement and demonstrate its impact
  • Prepares educators to apply research to decision making
  • Uses learning strategies appropriate to the intended goal
  • Applies knowledge about human learning and change
  • Provides educators with the knowledge and skills to collaborate
Content standards
  Staff development that improves the learning of all students:
  • Prepares educators to understand and appreciate all students; create safe, orderly, and supportive learning environments; and hold high expectations for their academic achievement
  • Deepens educators' content knowledge, provides them with research-based instructional strategies to assist students in meeting rigorous academic standards, and prepares them to use various types of classroom assessments appropriately
  • Provides educators with knowledge and skills to involve families and other stakeholders appropriately

---

Klingner, & Hughes, 2000), there is little in the way of scientific evidence that these consensus-based standards are effective at sustaining educational improvements.

More than just hoping that professional development can improve reading outcomes for struggling readers, we must enhance our knowledge base about precisely how that should happen. The simple answer to this dilemma is to encourage knowledge development on effective ways to enhance teacher knowledge and capacity for teaching struggling readers. To move us along toward this simple answer, I have proposed building on Gilbert's (1978) conceptual model of three system variables (data on valued and measurable outcomes; tools, materials, and technology; and incentives) and three personal variables (knowledge, capacity, and motivation) that would seem to be important for setting the occasion for successful professional development to be successful. In addition, I have proposed to add to this model the content of that professional development. Specifically, I believe professional development should focus on teachers' knowledge and capacity to teach reading with careful attention to teachers' psychological readiness to improve. In short, I believe the variables that should be studied stem directly from Gilbert's model applied to reading instruction.

With carefully designed, rigorously implemented research studies using a range of methodologies, we would expect to be able to draw important conclusions about hypotheses that have been advanced in the literature but lack evidence to support or refute them, including the following:

1. *Not all teachers should receive the same type, amount, or intensity of professional development.* This seems obvious. After all, one of the reasons why we have so many struggling readers in our schools has been our insistence on teaching all children the same content in the same classrooms for the same amount of time despite differences in their background knowledge, capacity, and interest in learning (Vaughn, Moody, & Schumm, 1998). Perhaps differentiated instruction for teachers with vastly different levels of knowledge, expertise, and capacity would be equally effective (Bos et al., 2001).

2. *Professional development content based on school-level reading outcomes leads to more effective practices and improved outcomes.* Because we have never attempted to monitor student reading performance across the grade levels on measures that predict later reading success, we have not had classroom-specific data with which to judge teachers' effectiveness. If these systems of assessment are in place, we could test the efficacy of professional development that is differentiated based on student performance (Good, Simmons, & Kame'enui, 2001).

3. *Teachers who receive professional development in reading pedagogy linked to specific core reading materials are more effective at teaching reading and sustain these effective practices longer than teachers who receive professional development unrelated to specific materials.* Many states (e.g., California) are spending large amounts of money on providing professional development that is program specific. This means that teachers are receiving detailed instruction on how to implement particular commercial reading programs. Little is known about the efficacy of this approach over a more general focus on reading instruction.

4. *Professional development is more effective when it is done as a schoolwide effort.* Although some efforts to study schoolwide approaches to professional development and reading improvement have been encouraging (e.g., Chard, Vaughn, Tyler, & Sloan, 2000; Kame'enui, Simmons, & Coyne, 2000), the empirical research in this area is underdeveloped. Questions regarding how to effectively differentiate professional development, monitor teachers' effectiveness, and improve instructional leadership and coaching remain unanswered.

5. *Teachers who work with students with reading disabilities require more extensive knowledge of language structure and specific instructional techniques designed to address specific strengths and deficits.* Because much research on instruction for students with specific reading disabilities has been conducted clinically or in the absence of effective instruction in general education classrooms, much remains to be learned about what should constitute professional development for teachers working with students with more intensive reading needs (Brady & Moats, 1997; Chard, 1999).

DISCUSSION

My intent in this article was to present a conceptual model of professional development for reading teachers in a much larger context than has traditionally been articulated. By using Gilbert's (1978) model of competence to guide our discussion of selected professional development literature, I suggest that the effectiveness and sustainability of professional development efforts may be inextricably linked to other school factors such as clear and measurable reading goals and well-designed instructional tools. In addition, I have described a system of professional development that delineates the enhancement of domain-specific and general pedagogical knowledge as well as teachers' capacity to apply their knowledge in the classroom. Finally, I linked professional development to the literature available on teachers' motivation to improve.

Admittedly, there is nothing unique about any one of these elements. My contention is that their interdependence may be the key to effective and sustainable improvement in student reading achievement. By most estimates, knowledgeable and effective teachers play a significant role in ensuring that students learn (Sanders & Rivers, 1996; Whitehurst, 2002). At present, we cannot explain with much confidence how to maximize teachers' potential to teach students to read, particularly those struggling to learn.

The research on what constitutes effective professional development is very limited (National Reading Panel, 2000). Developing our knowledge base about what professional development efforts will lead to improved reading outcomes for all students is essential.

REFERENCES

Adams, M. J. (1990). *Beginning to read: Thinking and learning about print.* Cambridge, MA: Academic.

Adams, M. J. (1999). The three cueing system. In J. Osborn & F. Lehr (Eds.), *Literacy for all* (pp. 73–99). New York: Guilford.

Armbruster, B. B., Lehr, F., & Osborn, J. (2001). *Put reading first: The research building blocks for teaching children to read.* Washington, DC: National Institute for Literacy.

Ashton, P. T., & Webb, R. B. (1986). *Making a difference: Teachers' sense of efficacy and student achievement.* New York: Longman.

Bandura, A. (1977). Self-efficacy: Toward a unifying theory of behavioral change. *Psychological Review, 84,* 191–215.

Beck, I. L., McKeown, M. G., Sandora, C., Kucan, L., & Worthy, J. (1996). Questioning the author: A yearlong classroom implementation to engage students with text. *The Elementary School Journal, 96,* 385–414.

Bos, C., Mather, N., Dickson, S., Podhajski, B., & Chard, D. (2001). Perceptions and knowledge of preservice and inservice educators about early reading instruction. *Annals of Dyslexia, 51,* 97–120.

Brabham, E. G., & Villaume, S. K. (2002). Leveled text: The good news and the bad news. *Reading Teacher, 55,* 438–441.

Brady, S., & Moats, L. (1997). *Informed instruction for reading success: Foundations for teacher preparation.* Baltimore: International Dyslexia Association.

Brophy, J. E. (1983). Research on the self-fulfilling prophecy and teacher expectations. *Journal of Educational Psychology, 75,* 631–681.

Chard, D. J. (1999). Improving teacher certification in reading for special educators. *Perspectives: The Newsletter of the International Dyslexia Association, 25*(4), 15–19.

Chard, D. J., & Kame'enui, E. J. (2000). Struggling first grade readers: The frequency and progress of their reading. *The Journal of Special Education, 34,* 28–38.

Chard, D. J., Vaughn, S., Tyler, B. J., & Sloan, K. (2000). Implementing a schoolwide model of reading improvement. *The Australasian Journal of Special Education, 12,* 21–34.

Commission on Reading. (1984). *Becoming a nation of readers.* Washington, DC: U.S. Department of Education.

Committee on the Prevention of Reading Difficulties. (1998). *Preventing reading difficulties in young children.* Washington, DC: National Academy Press.

Darling-Hammond, L., & Young, P. (2002). Defining "highly qualified teachers": What does "scientifically-based research" actually tell us? *Educational Researcher, 31,* 13–25.

Denham, C., & Michael, J. J. (1981). Teacher sense of efficacy: A definition of the construct and a model for further research. *Educational Research Quarterly, 5,* 39–63.

Dickson, S. V., & Bursuck, W. (2003). Implementing an outcomes-based collaborative partnership in preventing reading failure. In D. L. Wiseman & S. L. Knight (Eds.), *Linking school–university collaboration and K–12 student outcomes.* New York: American Association of Colleges for Teacher Education.

Ehri, L. (1995). Phases of development in learning to read words by sight. *Journal of Research in Reading, 18,* 116–125.

Elbaum, B., Vaughn, S., Hughes, M., & Moody, S. W. (1999). Grouping practices and reading outcomes for students with disabilities. *Exceptional Children, 65,* 399–415.

Elmore, R. F. (2002). *Bridging the gap between standards and achievement: The imperative for professional development in education.* Washington, DC: Albert Shanker Institute.

Foorman, B. F., Fletcher, J. M., Francis, D. J., Schatschneider, C., & Mehta, P. (1998). The role of instruction in learning to read: Preventing reading failure in at risk children. *Journal of Educational Psychology, 90,* 37–55.

Gersten, R., & Baker, S. (2001). Teaching expressive writing to students with learning disabilities: A meta-analysis. *Elementary School Journal, 101,* 251–272.

Gersten, R., Chard, D., & Baker, S. (2000). Factors enhancing sustained use of research-based instructional practices. *Journal of Learning Disabilities, 5,* 445–457.

Gersten, R., Fuchs, L. S., Williams, J., & Baker, S. (2001). Teaching reading comprehension to students with learning disabilities: A review of research. *Review of Educational Research, 71,* 279–320.

Gibson, S., & Dembo, M. H. (1984). Teacher efficacy: A construct validation. *Journal of Educational Psychology, 76,* 569–582.

Gilbert, T. E. (1978). *Human competence: Engineering worthy performance.* New York: McGraw-Hill.

Good, R. H., Simmons, D. C., & Kame'enui, E. J. (2001). The importance and decision-making utility of a continuum of fluency-based indicators of foundational reading skills for third-grade high-stakes outcomes. *Scientific Studies of Reading, 5,* 257–288.

Grossman, P. L., Valencia, S. W., & Hamel, F. (1995). Preparing language arts teachers in a time of reform. In J. Flood, S. B. Heath, & D. Lapp (Eds.), *Handbook for research on teaching literacy through the communicative and visual arts* (pp. 407–416). New York: Macmillan.

Gurney, D., Gersten, R., Dimino, J., & Carnine, D. (1990). Story grammar: Effective literature instruction for high school students with learning disabilities. *Journal of Learning Disabilities, 23,* 335–342.

Guskey, T. R. (1989). Attitude and perceptual change in teachers. *International Journal of Educational Research, 13,* 439–453.

Hoy, W. K., & Woolfolk, A. E. (1990). Socialization of student teachers. *American Educational Research Journal, 27,* 279–300.

Idol, L., & Croll, V. J. (1987). Story-mapping training as a means of improving reading comprehension. *Learning Disability Quarterly, 10,* 214–229.

Jitendra, A. K., Chard, D., Hoppes, M. K., Renouf, K., & Cardill, M. C. (2001). An evaluation of main idea strategy instruction in four commercial reading programs: Implications for students with learning problems. *Reading & Writing Quarterly: Overcoming Learning Difficulties, 17,* 53–73.

Juel, C. (1988). Learning to read and write: A longitudinal study of 54 children from first through fourth grades. *Journal of Educational Psychology, 80,* 437–447.

Kame'enui, E. J., Simmons, D. C., & Coyne, M. D. (2000). Schools as host environments: Toward a schoolwide reading improvement model. *Annals of Dyslexia, 50,* 33–51.

Kaminski, R. A., & Good, R. H. (1998). Assessing early literacy skills in a problem-solving model: Dynamic indicators of basic early literacy skills. In M. R. Shinn (Ed.), *Advanced applications of curriculum based measurement* (pp. 113–142). New York: Guilford.

Kennedy, M. M. (1991). Implications for teaching. In E. A. Ramp & C. S. Pederson (Eds.), *Follow through: Program and policy issues* (pp. 57–71). Washington, DC: U.S. Department of Education, Office of Education Research and Improvement.

Klingner, J. K., Vaughn, S., Hughes, M. T., & Arguelles, M. E. (1999). Sustaining research-based practices in reading: A 3-year follow-up. *Remedial and Special Education, 20,* 263–274.

Klingner, J. K., Vaughn, S., & Schumm, J. S. (1998). Collaborative strategic reading during social studies in heterogeneous fourth-grade classrooms. *Elementary School Journal, 99,* 3–22.

McCutchen, D., Harry, L., Cunningham, A. E., Cox, S., Sidman, S., & Covill, A. (2002). Content knowledge of teachers of beginning reading. *Annals of Dyslexia, 52,* 207–228.

Moats, L. C. (1994). The missing foundation in teacher education: Knowledge of the structure of spoken and written language. *Annals of Dyslexia, 44,* 81–102.

National Center for Educational Statistics. (2000). *The nation's report card.* Washington, DC: Author.

National Reading Panel. (2000). *Teaching children to read: An evidence based assessment of the scientific research literature on reading and its implications for reading instruction.* Bethesda, MD: National Institute of Child Health and Human Development.

National Research Council, Committee on Minority Representation in Special Education. (2002). *Minority students in special and gifted education.* Washington, DC: National Academy Press.

O'Connor, R. E., Jenkins, J. R., & Slocum, T. A. (1995). Transfer among phonological tasks in kindergarten: Essential instructional content. *Journal of Educational Psychology, 87,* 202–217.

Pressley, M., Wharton-McDonald, R., Allington, R., Block, C. C., Morrow, L., Tracey, D., et al. (2001). A study of effective grade-1 literacy instruction. *Scientific Studies of Reading, 5,* 35–58.

Rayner, K., Foorman, B. R., Perfetti, C. A., Pesetsky, D., & Seidenberg, M. S. (2001). How psychological science informs the teaching of reading. *Psychological Science in the Public Interest, 2,* 31–74.

Richardson, V. (Ed.). (1994). *Teacher change and the staff development process: A case in reading instruction.* New York: Teachers College Press.

Rosenshine, B. (1997). Advances in research on instruction. In J. W. Lloyd, E. J. Kame'enui, & D. Chard (Eds.), *Issues in educating students with disabilities* (pp. 197–220). Mahwah, NJ: Lawrence Erlbaum Associates, Inc.

Sanders, W., & Rivers, J. (1996). *Cumulative and residual effects of teachers on future student achievement.* Knoxville: University of Tennessee, Value-Added Research and Assessment Center.

Simmons, D. C., Kame'enui, E. J., & Chard, D. J. (1998). General education teachers' assumptions about learning and students with learning disabilities: Design-of-instruction analysis. *Learning Disability Quarterly, 21,* 6–21.

Smith, S., Simmons, D., Gleason, M. M., Kame'enui, E. J., Baker, S. K., Sprick, M., et al. (2001). An analysis of phonological awareness instruction in four kindergarten basal reading programs. *Reading & Writing Quarterly: Overcoming Learning Difficulties, 17,* 25–51.

Smylie, M. A. (1988). The enhancement function of staff development: Organizational and psychological antecedents to individual teacher change. *American Educational Research Journal, 25,* 1–30.

Swanson, H. L., & Hoskyn, M. (1998). Experimental intervention research on students with learning disabilities: A meta-analysis of treatment outcomes. *Review of Educational Research, 68,* 277–321.

Torgesen, J. K. (2003, March). *Scientific research and reading instruction for students with significant reading difficulties.* Paper presented at the Elissa Herst Teacher Training Forum, Princeton, NJ.

Torgesen, J. K., Alexander, A. W., Wagner, R. K., Rashotte, C. A., Voeller, K. K., & Conway, T. (2001). Intensive remedial instruction for children with severe reading disabilities: Immediate and long-term outcomes from two instructional approaches. *Journal of Learning Disabilities, 34,* 33–58.

Torgesen, J. K., Wagner, R. K., Rashotte, C. A., Rose, E., Lindamood, P., Conway, T., et al. (1999). Preventing reading failure in young children with phonological processing disabilities: Group and individual responses to instruction. *Journal of Educational Psychology, 91,* 579–593.

Vaughn, S., Klingner, J., & Hughes, M. (2000). Sustainability of research-based practices. *Exceptional Children, 66,* 163–171.

Vaughn, S., Moody, S. W., & Schumm, J. S. (1998). Broken promises: Reading instruction in the resource room. *Exceptional Children, 64,* 211–225.

Whitehurst, G. J. (2002, March). *Research on teacher preparation and professional development.* Paper presented at the White House Conference on Preparing Tomorrow's Teachers, Washington, DC.

Wong, B. Y. L. (2000). Writing strategies instruction for expository essays for adolescents with and without learning disabilities. *Topics in Language Disorders, 20,* 29–44.

www.ingramcontent.com/pod-product-compliance
Ingram Content Group UK Ltd.
Pitfield, Milton Keynes, MK11 3LW, UK
UKHW020427010325

9 780805 895322